MW01147821

THE LIFE OF CHRIST
VISUALIZED

THE LIFE OF CHRIST VISUALIZED

By

RAY E. BAUGHMAN, E.D.

Dean of External Studies
Dallas Bible College

Illustrated by
BRYAN LEE BAUGHMAN

ISBN: 0-8024-4726-0

1978 Printing

Printed in the United States of America

CONTENTS

APPENDIXES

CHAPTER 1

OUR GOAL AND METHOD OF STUDY

The life stories of David, Daniel, Joseph and Paul are familiar to all of us. But the life story of Jesus is much more difficult to retell. Since the events of Christ's earthly life are not treated identically in all the gospels, many people lack understanding of the historical times and places involved. Therefore they find it difficult to appreciate the inner relation between the various recorded events in Christ's life or to see the progressive development of God's plan. This book will follow the basic pattern of the author's previous book, *Bible History Visualized.** It will expand the section with the C-title, "The Cross," from that book.

This book is written to help you:

1. to see God revealed in Jesus Christ so that, as Paul says, you might "know him" as a person. Too often a Christian's view of Christ is just a figment of his own imagination, like an artist's drawing.

2. to see God's program unfold.

3. to outline each period of Christ's life so that you can follow Him from His birth to His ascension, placing each event chronologically and geographically.

4. to provide memory helps to make the retention of these events as easy as possible—or as some say, "hard to forget."

5. to provide a simple method of marking the New Testament so that the material studied in this course will be reviewed any time you use your Bible. This course will become the foundation on which extra material can be added in the future.

*Published by Moody Press, Chicago, Ill., 1963.

6. to provide important background information.

SUGGESTED USES OF THIS BOOK

This material has been taught for six years at the Dallas Bible College, in Sunday schools, in training unions and at Bible conferences. It has been put in its present form so it can be used for these study groups, home Bible classes or individual use. Extra reports by class members have proved an interesting addition to class study. The following recommended topics can be studied in a Bible dictionary: customs of the people and times, geographical facts, secular history, the temple, houses and dwellings, trades and occupations. The following reports can be made by reading the gospel accounts, collecting all the references, and organizing them into reports such as: Christ and social life, Christ and demons, Christ and children, Christ's companions, Christ's healing ministry, teaching, miracles, prayer life. Other reports can be made from the appendixes in this book.

DISPUTED PASSAGES

It is not the goal of this book to solve disputed textual, chronological or theological problems but to see Christ in His earthly ministry as He moves among mankind, to follow Him from the cradle to the cross, and to watch Him as He ascends into heaven.

HARMONY OF THE GOSPELS

The harmony used in this book is not new. It is based upon the four-passover view of Christ's ministry. The work of previous scholars is acknowledged: A. T Robertson, John A. Broadus, John H. Kerr, W. A. Stevens and E. D. Burton, and many others, extending back to the early days of the church. Following the general chronology of the standard harmonies, the author has divided Christ's life story so it will fit a special chart. There are about one hundred twenty distinguishable incidents in the life of Christ. Some are mentioned only with a phrase or a few words, and it is hard to know whether the Bible is recording different events or events mentioned in more detail in other gospels.

It is important to understand that the gospel accounts are basically in chronological order. None of the Gospels record everything, but the things they do record are in order with a few minor exceptions. The big exception is in Matthew 8-12. The events in these chapters are grouped by themes.

DATES

Opinions vary as to the dates involved in the life of Christ. We will use 5 B.C. for the birth of Christ, A.D. 26 for the beginning of His ministry, and A.D. 30 for His death. If you prefer to use a different date, such as 4 B.C. for His birth, you will have to adjust the other dates accordingly. The traditional Friday crucifixion date will be used, although there are good reasons to believe that He was crucified earlier in the week. If so, the order of events would be the same, but the days would be different.

SIMILAR EVENTS AND REPEATED SAYINGS

There are two things which cause difficulty in keeping the chronology of the life of Christ straight: similar events and repeated sayings. For example, Jesus cleansed the temple twice. One cleansing was at the beginning of His ministry, and the other was in the final week.

The other problem is the repeated sayings of Christ. Jesus sometimes used the same illustration or brought the same message to people in different localities. There are many similarities between His ministry in Galilee and His later ministry in Peraea. For instance, faith is compared to a mustard seed in Galilee (Matt. 17:20) and in Peraea (Luke 17:6).

READING ASSIGNMENT

At the beginning of each section the Scripture references will be given which record that particular part of the life of Christ. It will be very profitable to read all the references because almost invariably other details will be given in the parallel accounts. You are to study Christ's life from the Bible for no attempt will be made to retell the life of Christ in narrative style. It is recommended that you mark your New Testament according to the method given in Appendix C before you start reading.

APPENDIXES

In the back of the book are several appendixes in which additional information has been given. Some of the material concerns several events from different periods of Christ's ministry. For example: the synagogue, weddings, scribes, eating customs.

TIME CHART OF THE MINISTRY OF CHRIST

The author is indebted to a friend, Dan England, for the basic idea of dividing the ministry of Christ in this manner. If you've ever watched a postal clerk sorting mail, you will remember how he quickly sorts the mail into the various pigeon holes or boxes according to the address. This idea will be used to help you remember the order of events in the life of Christ.

The chart you will use resembles a school schedule. The right-hand column represents the fall semester of the year, the left-hand column the spring semester, and the center column the summer vacation. This allows you to divide the year into periods of about four months each.

The divisions between the periods are determined by the feasts of Israel. The vertical line between the spring of the year and the summer vacation represents the Passover Feast. This usually occurs in April. The line between the summer vacation and the fall semester represents the Feast of Tabernacles which usually occurs in September. The line between the fall and spring semesters (the line on each side of the chart) represents the Feast of Dedication which takes place in late December.

TIME CHART FOR THE LIFE OF CHRIST

The ministry of Christ can be compared to a school schedule:

Spring Semester	Summer Vacation	Fall Semester
5 B.C. to A.D. 26 BABIES		Fall A.D. 26 SEE
Spring 27 C. C.	Summer 27 FFNJJ	Fall 27 WELL
Spring 28 BLDG.	Summer 28 MAN	Fall 28 SEA
Spring 29 212.	Summer 29 FOOD	Fall 29 SERVING
Spring 30 TRAVEL	Final Week F. W.	Post Resurrection P. R.

↑ Feast of Dedication

↑ Feast of Passover (usually in April)

↑ Feast of Tabernacles (usually in September)

↑ Feast of Dedication

The Gospels do not record each of these feasts each year. Sometimes the events listed in a specific box occur very close to the end of that period, and the events occurring in the next box come very close to the beginning of that period. In a few instances it would be hard to say exactly which period the event should be in. This, however, is no great obstacle because we are still getting the events in their chronological order and within perhaps three months of the time they occurred.

11

The box at the beginning and the two at the end of the chart that are enclosed with broken lines are used to gather together events that occurred over different lengths of time. The one at the beginning records the time from the birth of Christ until He begins His ministry thirty years later. The one in the center column at the bottom is the final week before Christ is crucified. The final box in the right-hand column covers the period of forty days from the resurrection of Christ to His ascension.

MEMORY HELPS

In each of the boxes or periods you will use a key word to help relate the events to one another. Abbreviations will also be used to indicate the time period for each box. For example, the fall of the year A.D. 26 will be indicated by F-26, the spring of the year A.D. 27 by Sp-27, and the summer of the year A.D. 28 by the symbol S-28.

Additional memory helps will be given in each period as you study.

The events in each period will sometimes be clustered in groups of two to four events with the emphasis put upon one key event. The events will have some relationship with each other: happen at about the same time, or in the same place, or deal with the same subject.

A small chart will be given at the start of each section with a dot to indicate what period you are in. For example, in the summer of 28, it will look like this:

Most of the appendixes are also listed alphabetically. For example:

Appendix A—Angels
Appendix B—Buildings
Appendix C—Chronology

12

REVIEW TESTS

You may take the review tests any time you feel you are ready for them. If this book is being studied by a class, the teacher may want to use them to promote class participation or discussion. Little flashcards are very helpful for personal or class study. On one side put the event, for example, the baptism of Jesus. On the other side put the key word and time period: SEE, F-26. Shuffle the cards and then see if you can tell in what period the event occurred.

CHAPTER 2

WHAT IS GOD'S PURPOSE?

A man was walking through his garden one day and he noticed some ants busily working in his flower bed. The anthill was located in a place that he intended to cultivate. All the work the ants were doing was useless and would be

destroyed. But how could he tell the ants? They couldn't understand if he spoke to them; they couldn't read; it was hopeless. If only he could become an ant, then he could tell them, and they would understand. This simple illustration helps explain why God "became flesh" (John 1:14, ASV). Since Adam sinned in the garden, man's knowledge of God has been clouded. The downward path of spiritual ignorance is traced in Romans 1:21-23. Man's sin has separated him from God. The Bible describes man as lost and under condemnation (Rom. 6:23; John 3:16-18). But Jesus said, "For the Son of man is come to seek and to save that which was lost" (Luke 19:10), "and to give his life a ransom for many" (Matt. 20:28; I Tim. 2:5-6). You see, "God was in Christ, reconciling the world unto himself" (II Cor. 5:19). "God was manifest [revealed] in the flesh" (I Tim. 3:16).

Man's standard of righteousness has also been perverted. He doesn't understand what kind of conduct would be required in order to have fellowship and communion with God. Jesus Christ through His holy life gave the perfect example of what God requires. When men see themselves in contrast

14

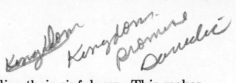

to Jesus, it makes them realize their sinfulness. This makes them understand their need for a Saviour. Peter said, "I am a sinful man, O Lord" (Luke 5:8).

Jesus came to Israel offering the kingdom promised in the Old Testament (e.g., II Sam. 7:8-17).

In Jesus' ministry there is a blending of two Old Testament promises concerning the Messiah, or the Christ: His provision of salvation (Isa. 53:1-12) and His reign as King (Isa. 2:1-12). Some of the self-righteous Jews would have accepted Jesus as King, but they wouldn't receive Him as Saviour (John 1:11-12; cf. 6:15). God foresaw their rejection and caused the very wrath of man to be overruled for good as Jesus died for the sins of the world (I John 2:2).

From the beginning Satan has tried to confuse and deceive man about God's true character and lead man into rebellion against God (Gen. 3:1-5). But "for this purpose the Son of God was manifested, that he might destroy the works of the devil" (I John 3:8).

Jesus is called "Emmanuel, which being interpreted is, God with us" (Matt. 1:23). Remember, Jesus didn't come into being at Bethlehem—He is eternal (John 1:1). But He took on human flesh, was born as a baby, and grew up into manhood (Luke 2:52). He is unique and different from all others in that He is the God-man: truly God and truly man.

The life of Christ has these major themes running through it:

1. Jesus revealing what God is like.
2. Jesus revealing through His life God's perfect standard for men.
3. Jesus providing redemption from sin.
4. Jesus destroying the works of the devil.
5. Jesus offering the kingdom to Israel.
6. Jesus being received and rejected as Messiah. His

rejection introduced two minor themes: His second coming and the establishment of the church.

THE KINGDOM OF GOD

Since God created the earth and all of the universe, there is a sense in which His kingdom is composed of the entire universe. He rules sovereignly over it and does what He wants with it. In His wisdom He has allowed man to exercise his will. He did not force each part of His creation to do certain things whether they desired to or not. Man chose to rebel against the will of God, and he is responsible for his own sin. Man is a rebel in God's universe. He came under the penalty of sin. Man's first and greatest need is to be redeemed from the penalty of this sin so that he can re-enter the kingdom as a son of God. He is still under the rule of God but as a condemned criminal.

USE OF THE WORD KINGDOM

The word *kingdom* is used in the Bible in three different ways:

1. The *realm* or territory that is ruled (Matt. 4:8; 6:13; 24:7; Luke 4:5).

2. The *people* that are ruled (Matt. 6:33, the people who accepted God's rule of their lives; 21:31; Mark 10:15; Luke 16:16; Col. 1:13). At other times the word is used because the kingdom is present in the person of the King (Matt. 12:28; Luke 17:21).

3. The *reign* or rule itself. Sometimes the time factor—such as twenty years—is meant (Luke 19:12; 22:29; I Cor. 15:24-26).

Although the matter is much debated, the two expressions "the kingdom of God" and "the kingdom of heaven" as used in the Gospels seem to be talking about the same thing. The term "kingdom of heaven" is a Jewish term used in the Old Testament. In Daniel 2:44 it is used of a kingdom that is set up on earth but comes from heaven or has its origin in heaven.

16

A DEFINITION

The kingdom of God is the rule of God in Christ:

1. Over a redeemed people who have received Him.

2. In which Satan and the forces of evil are defeated.

3. Which issues into a realm or territory on earth in which the power of His reign is experienced.

The kingdom of God will pass through three phases:

1. The kingdom has been given to Jesus Christ the Son.

2. John the Baptist and Jesus and His disciples announced that the kingdom of God was at hand and invited the people to enter in. This was a personal invitation. Entrance was gained through the new birth (John 1:12-13; 3:3-5).

3. God had promised Israel in the Davidic Covenant a literal kingdom. He even gave the dimensions of it, from the Mediterranean Sea to the Euphrates River and southwest to the river of Egypt (Gen. 15:18; Ezek. 48:1-28). This is about eight times as large a territory as the twelve tribes occupied.

The kingdom promised Israel will be for one thousand years, a millennium. At the end of this time the heavens and earth will be renovated. The Scriptures talk about a new heaven and a new earth (Rev. 21:1). When this happens, the kingdom of God will assume its eternal character. As you read, you must tell by the context or the whole passage what the Scriptures mean when they use the term "kingdom of God." Are they talking about the rule or reign itself, the people God rules, or the realm or land in which He rules?

BASIC OBJECTIVE

The object of the kingdom of God is the redemption and deliverance of the people of this world from the power of evil and the curse of sin. This of course includes death which is called the last enemy (I Cor. 15:23-28). This is an invasion of enemy territory. The kingdoms of this world are under Satan (Matt. 4:8-9; Luke 4:5-6; II Cor. 4:4).

In the first part of the Old Testament the emphasis is placed on the redemptive work of the coming Saviour (Gen. 3:15). Kings are just mentioned to Abraham (Gen. 17:5-7) and to Jacob (Gen. 35:11; 49:10), and later in Balaam's prophecy (Num. 24:17). After the period of the judges when the children of Israel had returned to the land, God gave them a king, Saul (I Sam. 12:13). It was with King David that God made an unconditional, eternal covenant (II Sam. 7:8-17). It was with David's throne and lineage that the promised King and kingdom were identified. The expression used in the New Testament, "son of David," refers to this covenant.

When the nation was taken captive into Babylon and all looked like it was lost, God gave Nebuchadnezzar his dream of the great image. The fifth kingdom in this dream, as interpreted by Daniel with the Lord's help, is a kingdom that has its origin in heaven. This kingdom of heaven will be set up by God. Almost all of the Old Testament prophets referred to the coming kingdom. Isaiah 40:1-11; 60:1-21; Jeremiah 31:1-37; Ezekiel 34:20-31; Hosea 3:4-5; Joel 2:28—3:2; Micah 4:1—5:5; and Zechariah 2:1-13; 6:11-13 are a few of the many references about the kingdom. Obadiah, Amos, Zephaniah and Malachi as well as many of the psalms give additional details of the promised kingdom. The Jews living during the ministry of Christ had some distorted ideas about the promised kingdom. However, they were looking for a literal kingdom as promised in the Old Testament.

God had recorded many promises of redemption and deliverance in His Word. Israel was given the task of looking after that Word (Rom. 3:2). The scribes in their interpretations had "taken away the key of knowledge" (Luke 11:52) so the keys of the kingdom of heaven were given to the disciples (Matt. 16:19). The key is faith in Jesus Christ as the Son of God, the Messiah, the Saviour. This is the only way into the kingdom.

The teaching concerning the kingdom in the Old Testament can be summarized as follows:

18

1. *God will be King.* His name will be "Emmanuel, . . . God with us" (Matt. 1:23). By human birth He will be of the lineage of David (II Sam. 7:16). He will be born of a virgin (Isa. 7:14) in Bethlehem (Micah 5:2).

2. *Jerusalem will be His capital* (Isa. 2:1-3; 62:1-7).

3. *He will rule over regathered and converted Israel* (Deut. 30:3-6; Isa. 11:11-12; Jer. 23:6-8; 33:7-9).

4. *His kingdom will be given to Israel, but it will extend over other nations of the earth as well.* They will pay tribute to Christ (Ps. 72:11, 17; Isa. 55:5; Dan. 7:13-14; Zech. 8:22).

5. *His kingdom will be characterized by righteousness and holiness.* It will bring forgiveness of sins, a new heart, a knowledge of God, the outpouring of the Spirit of God upon all flesh, inward harmony to the laws of God in contrast to an outward conformity, and the restoring of joy to the human life (Isa. 35:10; Jer. 31:28-34; Ezek. 36:24-28; Zech. 8:20-23).

6. *He will bring social changes.* War will be eliminated. Worldwide peace will come, and there will be justice for all (Ps. 72:1-14; Isa. 65:21-22; Zech. 9:10).

7. *He will bring changes in nature.* People will live longer. Disease will be abolished. There will be climatic changes with a great increase of the productivity of the soil and no famine (Isa. 11:6-9; 32:14-16; 35:5-6; 65:20, 22; Ezek. 36:24-36).

8. *Satan will be bound* (Rev. 20:2). Near the end of the millennium Satan will be loosed for a little season before he is finally judged and cast into the lake of fire and brimstone with his fallen angels.

9. *The Old Testament saints will be raised* (Jer. 30:9; Ezek. 37:24-25; Luke 13:28). The Old Testament saints to whom God promised the kingdom will be resurrected and have a part in the kingdom.

10. *The church is not the kingdom.* Jesus spoke of the church as being yet in the future in Matthew 16:18. It is a called-out body of believers composed of both Jews and

19

Gentiles. It is the body of Christ (Eph. 5:25-32), a joint heir with Christ (Rom. 8:17), a royal priesthood (I Peter 2:9; Rev. 1:6). The church will hold and exercise certain judicial authority with Christ (I Cor. 6:2-4; 15:28; II Tim. 2:12; Rev. 5:10).

These facts or their distortions (with the exception of church truth) made up the kingdom background knowledge of the people to whom Jesus came.

CHAPTER 3

BIRTH OF CHRIST

5 B.C. TO A.D. 26

KEY WORD: BABIES

INTRODUCTION: Matthew 1:1-25; Luke 1:1-80; John 1:1-13.

Key Events	Matthew	Luke	John
1. **B** irth at Bethlehem, shepherds, angels		2:1-20	1:14
2. **A** doration of Simeon and Anna (Jerusalem) and the wise men (Bethlehem)	2:1-12	2:21-38	
3. **B** ethlehem babies killed	2:16-18		
4. **I** nto Egypt (flight of Mary, Joseph and Jesus)	2:13-15		
5. **E** gyptian exile ended, return to Nazareth ·	2:19-23	2:39-40	
6. **S** earch for Jesus (12 years old, visit to temple in Jerusalem)		2:41-52	

Read at least the fullest account of each event. Read them in the order given.

Locate each of the key events on the maps in Appendix G.

Mary and Joseph brought the Baby Jesus into the court of the women. This is probably the place where Anna and Simeon would see Him. When Jesus was talking with the doctors or scribes, it was probably in Solomon's porch. Find these locations on the temple diagram in Appendix B.

HOW COULD THEY KNOW JESUS WAS THE MESSIAH?

Sometimes today a messenger or agent will carry with him a letter of introduction, identification papers, or some other kind of credentials. Sometimes a description of him will be sent on ahead so that he will be recognized when he comes. This is true of Christ: all through the Old Testament God gave details about the coming Saviour. In fact, one could have almost filled out a birth certificate in advance.

BIRTH CERTIFICATE OF THE MESSIAH

Name: *Jesus (Matt. 1:21), Immanuel (Isa. 7:14) many others (Isa. 9:6)*

Race: *Human (Gen. 3:15), not an animal or other created being (Heb. 10:4)*

Nation: Hebrew *(Gen. 12:2; 18:18)*   Tribe: *Judah (Gen. 49:10)*

Family: *David (II Sam. 7:16-17)*

Parents: *Virgin Mary (Isa. 7:14); (Luke 1:27-35)*
Holy Spirit (Matt. 1:20, 22-23)

Place of birth: *Bethlehem (Micah 5:2)*

Sign in nature: *Star (Num. 24:17; Matt. 2:9-10)*

Date of birth: *5 B.C. (approximate time given in Dan. 9:26)*

Witnesses who saw the Baby Jesus: *Angels (Luke 2:11)*
Shepherds (Luke 2:16-17)

Throughout Jesus' ministry He continued to fulfill the things prophesied of Him and to perform miracles and do other things to show that He was God. He so lived that He could tell Philip, "He that hath seen me hath seen the Father" (John 14:9).

THE KING IS BORN

The angel Gabriel came to Mary before Jesus was born

and announced to her that the Child which she would bear would be called the Son of the Most High, that God had given unto Him the throne of His father David, that He would reign over the house of Jacob forever, and that of His kingdom there would be no end.

An angel appeared unto Joseph in a dream and told him that the Child which Mary would bear was conceived by the Holy Ghost and that He would save "his people" from their sins. The record of Jesus' royal lineage is recorded in Matthew 1 and Luke 3.

Jesus was born in the city of David, Bethlehem. The angel of the Lord told the shepherds, "For unto you is born this day in the city of David a Saviour, which is Christ the Lord" (Luke 2:11). The angels praised God saying, "Glory to God in the highest, and on earth peace, good will toward men" (Luke 2:14). Peace is one of the characteristics of the promised kingdom.

When the wise men came they asked, "Where is he that is born king of the Jews?" (Matt. 2:2). Herod was very troubled and all Jerusalem with him. He gathered the scribes and chief priests and asked where Christ should be born. They told him in Bethlehem (Micah 5:1-2). When the wise men found Jesus, they fell down and worshiped Him and presented gifts to Him. This foreshadows the worship of the nations of the world in the millennial kingdom of Christ (Ps. 86:9; Isa. 66:23; Zech. 14:16-19).

RECEPTION AND REJECTION OF CHRIST

Old Simeon in the temple recognized Jesus as the Saviour: "For mine eyes have seen thy salvation, . . . a light to lighten the Gentiles, and the glory of thy people Israel. . . . Behold, this child is set for the fall and rising again of many in Israel" (Luke 2:30-34). The most important question of all times is "What think ye of Jesus?" Is He the *Lord* who has taken on human flesh and become the Messiah? Was He a *lunatic* who was self-deceived and just thought He was God? Or was He a *liar* and a blasphemer who deliberately tried to deceive the people? Today, as during His earthly ministry, people have to make a choice: He is either the *Lord,* a *lunatic,* or a *liar.* Some would like to excuse themselves by saying, "I don't know," but their very refusal to believe the evidence is a rejection of Him as *Lord.*

In this first period you can see those who received Him as the promised Saviour: Mary and Joseph by faith even before He was born (see Appendix W), the shepherds, Simeon, Anna, and the wise men.

He was rejected by King Herod, his chief priests and scribes, and many of the people. When the wise men came inquiring about Jesus, all Jerusalem was troubled (Matt. 2:3), but apparently no one walked the five miles to Bethlehem to find Him.

MEMORY HELPS

There were two important babies born during this period: John the Baptist and Jesus. The key word for this period is

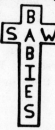

BABIES. The first letters from each of the key events spell out the word *babies.* The letter *A* stands for the adoration of Simeon, Anna, and the wise men. The first letters from each of these worshipers (Simeon, Anna, wise men) spell *saw.* They saw not just a baby but the promised Messiah.

WHAT GOD IS LIKE

His power: He caused the most powerful person in the world, the pagan Emperor Caesar Augustus, to put things in motion so that the plan of Messiah's birth would be according to God's plan (Gal. 4:4-5). He can cause the very stars of heaven to appear and to travel according to His bidding. The angels are His messengers and are subject to Him. He is all-powerful.

His faithfulness: God keeps His promises—He sent the Messiah.

24

His knowledge: He knows all things—past, present and future: He knew that Christ would be born in Bethlehem; He knew about the evil intentions of King Herod; and He knew exactly how He would protect Jesus and His family (Hosea 11:1). Nothing is hid from Him.

His grace: He showed His grace toward His two faithful old servants, Simeon and Anna, by allowing them to see the promised Messiah before they died.

His glory: The glory of the Lord shone round about the shepherds, and the angels praised God saying, "Glory to God in the highest."

His holiness: From His birth Jesus was called "holy" (Luke 1:35). He must be holy if He is God and the Saviour of lost mankind. If He had sinned, He would have deserved to be punished Himself.

His humility: God the Son "took upon him the form of a servant, and was made in the likeness of men" (Phil. 2:5-8; Heb. 10:5). As the perfect Man, He was also subject to His parents (Luke 2:51).

As you read, look for other things the Scripture tells about God.

QUESTIONS FOR MEDITATION

1. Is your heart as yielded to the Lord as Mary's was when she said, "Be it unto me according to thy word"?
2. Have you examined and accepted the credentials of the Word of God concerning the Saviour?
3. Do you adore and worship Him the way you should? Are you sometimes like the people of Jerusalem who felt they were too busy or it was too much effort to go to Bethlehem to seek Him?
4. Jesus revealed God's standard for the relation between parents and children; He was subject to His parents. Do you have the proper respect and honor for your parents?

See Appendixes A, B and H.

CHAPTER 4

CHRIST BEGINS
HIS MINISTRY

FALL OF A.D. 26

KEY WORD: SEE

INTRODUCTION: Matthew 3:1-12; Mark 1:1-8; Luke 3:1-18.

Key Events	Matthew	Mark	Luke	John
1. Baptism of Jesus (Jordan River)	3:13-17	1:9-11	3:21-23	
2. Temptation (Wilderness of Judaea)	4:1-11	1:12-13	4:1-13	
3. Testimony of John the Baptist (Jordan) —to religious delegation				1:15-28
—to his disciples				1:29-34
4. Jesus' first five disciples (Jordan)				1:35-51

Read at least the fullest account of each event. Read the accounts in their chronological order.

Locate each of the key events on the map. John was baptizing in the Jordan River, probably just above the Dead Sea. Traditionally this is the same place where Joshua crossed the Jordan with the children of Israel. The temptation of Christ probably took place in the wilderness of Judaea just northwest of the Dead Sea. The first disciples met the Lord after His temptation on the Jordan River at the place where John was baptizing.

26

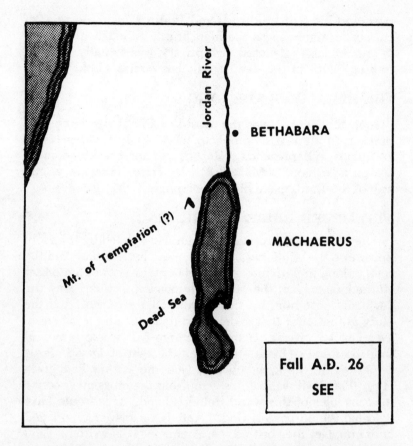

Jordan River

● BETHABARA

Mt. of Temptation (?)

● MACHAERUS

Dead Sea

Fall A.D. 26
SEE

It seems that this was very near the end of the year 26 A.D. and that they immediately returned to Galilee, probably up the Jordan Valley.

JESUS BEGINS HIS MINISTRY

When Jesus was about thirty years old, He began His earthly ministry. This was A.D. 26, the fifteenth year of Tiberius Caesar's rule of the Roman Empire. Pontius Pilate began His rule as governor of Judaea and Samaria also in A.D. 26. Herod Antipas was the tetrarch of Galilee and Pe-

27

raea, and his half brother Herod Philip II was the ruler of Ituraea. Caiaphas was the high priest, although his father-in-law, Annas (a deposed high priest), was actually the controlling figure in the Jewish religious circles (Luke 3:1-2).

THE HERALD OF THE KING

John the Baptist was the herald of Christ the King. He came in fulfillment of prophecy (Isa. 40:3-5). John came to Judaea and preached, "Repent ye: for the kingdom of heaven is at hand" (Matt. 3:2). He cried, "Prepare ye the way of the Lord, make his paths straight" (Mark 1:3).

ATTEMPTED BRIBE OF THE KING

After Jesus was baptized by John, He was led by the Holy Spirit into the wilderness to be tempted by Satan. "And the devil, taking him up into an high mountain, shewed unto him all the kingdoms of the world in a moment of time. And the devil said unto him, All this power will I give thee, and the glory of them: for that is delivered unto me; and to whomsoever I will I give it. If thou therefore wilt worship me, all shall be thine" (Luke 4:5-7). As the Son of David, Jesus came to rule the kingdom that God the Father had given Him. The devil wanted Jesus to avoid the cross and receive the kingdoms of this world from his hand. This would have defeated the purpose of God. "And Jesus answered and said unto him, Get thee behind me, Satan: for it is written, Thou shalt worship the Lord thy God, and him only shalt thou serve" (Luke 4:8).

THE MESSIAH: LAMB OF GOD AND KING OF
ISRAEL

After Jesus returned, John pointed Him out as the Lamb of God (John 1:29). When John's disciple Andrew found Jesus, he went to find his brother Simon and told him that he had found "the Messiah." Philip told Nathanael that they had found Him of whom Moses and the prophets wrote.

When Nathanael came to Jesus and Jesus told him that He had seen him sitting under the fig tree, "Nathanael answered and saith unto him, Rabbi, thou art the Son of God; thou art the King of Israel" (John 1:49).

JESUS THE PERFECT MAN

Jesus identified Himself with the people by asking John to baptize Him. Perhaps this also symbolized His anointing as King (I Sam. 16:13). In the Old Testament, oil represented the Holy Spirit. As Jesus was baptized, the Holy Spirit descended upon Him. He lived and fulfilled His earthly ministry as the Spirit-filled Son of God. The reason Jesus gave John for baptizing Him was to "fulfil all righteousness" —or to do all that was right. A perfect man does not just abstain from evil, but he does the good things he should. It was in this period that the first mention was made of Jesus' prayer life (Luke 3:21).

The Spirit of God led Jesus into the wilderness, and Satan tempted Him in all points (Heb. 4:15), but He did not yield. A Saviour must be sinless or He would deserve to be punished for His own sins and could not save others. So Jesus was put to the test—and He was victorious in temptation. A perfect man should have a knowledge of the Word of God (Matt. 4:7) and be led by the Holy Spirit (Matt. 4:1; Luke 4:1).

RECEPTION AND REJECTION OF CHRIST

John the Baptist and the five disciples received Jesus, but the religious committee from Jerusalem evidently was not interested enough to investigate John's testimony.

MEMORY HELPS

The key word of this section is SEE.

1. John *saw* the Holy Ghost descending upon Jesus.

2. During the temptation, Satan pointed out (*see*) the stones and asked Jesus to turn them into bread. Then he *showed* Him all the kingdoms of the world.

29

3. John pointed out Jesus by saying, "Behold the lamb of God." (The word *behold* in Greek can be translated "see.")

4. As Jesus met and called His first five disciples, He used the word *see* at least five times. Can you find them?

NOTICE: God allowed John the Baptist to use his eyes to *see* the sign which God had promised him (John 1:32-34). The devil tried to use the eyes as a means of tempting Jesus. The disciples used their eyes to *see* the Messiah. And Jesus in turn promised them that they would *see* wonderful things in the future (John 1:50-51).

WHAT GOD IS LIKE

His trinity: At Christ's baptism God was seen as a triune being: God the Father speaking from heaven, God the Holy Spirit descending as a dove, and God the Son.

His holiness: God the Father testified that He was pleased with Christ when He presented Himself for baptism. He was tempted in the wilderness, but did not sin.

His redemption: Jesus was identified as the promised Old Testament Lamb of God (Gen. 22:8; Exodus 12; Isa. 53:7).

His omniscience: Jesus exhibited His omniscience or knowledge of all things when He told Nathanael about being under the fig tree.

QUESTIONS FOR MEDITATION

1. The Lord had victory over temptation by the Spirit of God and the Word of God. Do you often yield to temptation because you do not use the same means?
2. John the Baptist, instead of attracting attention and followers to himself, pointed them to Jesus. Do you do the same?
3. Andrew brought his brother to Jesus, and Philip brought his friend Nathanael. Is there a member in your family or a friend that you should point to Jesus?

See Appendix O.

30

CHAPTER 5

CHRIST'S FIRST MIRACLE

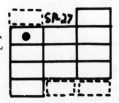

SPRING OF A.D. 27

KEY WORD: C.C.

Key Events	John
1. Cana, changing water to wine (first miracle)	2:1-11
2. Capernaum (first sojourn at future home)	2:12

Locate these two cities on the map in Appendix G.

CANA

After returning to Galilee, Jesus attended a wedding at Cana, about five miles north of Nazareth. This is one of a number of social occasions He attended that are mentioned in the Bible. His mother and His disciples were also with Him. God honored Mary above all women in that she should be the mother of Jesus, yet today many exalt her to unscriptural heights, calling her "the mother of God."

In this instance at Cana we have the only commandment recorded in the Scriptures that Mary ever gave: "Whatsoever he [Jesus] saith unto you, do it" (John 2:5). Jesus here performed the first miracle of His ministry by turning water into wine. In a very short time Jesus had been made known in three ways: (1) by the testimony of John the Baptist, (2) through His self-revelation to His disciples, and

31

(3) by His miracle at Cana where He "manifested . . . his glory."

John says that this is the first miracle ("sign-miracle" in Greek) that Jesus did. Again we see God revealing Himself to mankind; and the Scriptures say, "His disciples believed on him."

CAPERNAUM

Jesus then visited Capernaum which is on the northwest shore of the Sea of Galilee. It became the headquarters for much of His ministry, and many important events took place there.

THE KING PERFORMS A MIRACLE

One of the characteristics of the kingdom will be the fruitfulness of the earth. There will be no shortages of food. It seems as though Mary, recognizing Jesus as the Messiah, the King of Israel, believed that He could meet the shortage of wine at the wedding feast, and so she told Him about the need. The miracles He performed are in four categories: (1) miracles of physical healing, (2) miracles of resurrection, (3) miracles over evil spirits, and (4) miracles over nature. This is His first miracle over nature (see Appendix M).

MEMORY HELPS

In this period Jesus Christ, the Creator, was in two cities, Cana and Capernaum. Creator, Cana and Capernaum all begin with the letter C.

WHAT GOD IS LIKE

The Creator: The God who created all things (Col. 1:16) turned water into wine.

The Compassionate One: Jesus helped meet this material need at the wedding and used it as a sign-miracle for the servants. It also strengthened the faith of His disciples.

QUESTIONS FOR MEDITATION

1. Mary said, "Whatsoever he saith unto you, do it." Is it possible for Christ to manifest His glory in and through you because of your obedience?
2. Do you really believe that Christ is concerned about your needs?
3. Do you really believe that Christ is able to do something about your needs?

See Appendixes W, F and V.

CHAPTER 6

YOU MUST BE BORN AGAIN

SUMMER OF A.D. 27

KEY WORD: FFNJJ

Key Events	Matthew	Mark	Luke	John
1. **F**irst Passover during ministry (Jerusalem)				2:13
2. **F**irst cleansing of temple (Jerusalem)				2:14-25
3. **N**icodemus' interview, new birth (Jerusalem)				3:1-21
4. **J**udaean ministry of John and Jesus				3:22-26
5. **J**esus leaves Judaea as John is imprisoned (Machaerus)	4:12	1:14	3:19-20	4:1-4

FIRST PASSOVER

In this period Jesus attended the first Passover of four that occur during His ministry. It was at this first Passover that He first cleansed the temple. The Lord of the temple entered the temple of the Lord, and He was very angry with what He found. Various things had been brought into the temple area under the probable excuse of being necessary for worship; but Josephus, the Jewish historian, recorded the fact that many were getting rich from this practice, espe-

34

cially the high priest's family. (See the temple diagram in Appendix B.)

The Jewish authorities did not question whether it was right or wrong, but only by what authority Jesus had done this. This was His first challenge. In His reply, He gave them the first prophecy of His death and resurrection: "Destroy this temple, and in three days I will raise it up" (John 2:19). However, it wasn't understood by the authorities or by His disciples until after He arose from the grave.

NEW BIRTH

Right at the beginning of His public ministry, Jesus taught that all "must be born again." He went back into the Old Testament and showed how the things recorded there prefigured His ministry. Again He foretold His death when He said, "Even so must the Son of man be lifted up" (John 3:14).

ENTRANCE INTO THE KINGDOM

When Nicodemus came to Jesus and acknowledged that He was a teacher come from God because of the miracles that He performed, Jesus said unto him, "Verily, verily, I say unto thee, Except a man be born again, he cannot see the kingdom of God. . . . Except a man be born of water and of the Spirit, he cannot enter into the kingdom of God" (John 3:3-5). Nicodemus did not understand what this meant; and Jesus told him, "That which is born of the flesh is flesh; and that which is born of the Spirit is spirit" (John 3:6). Jesus explained to him that His mission was not to condemn the world but that the world through Him might be saved. Although Jesus came as the king of Israel, He came as Saviour to the whole world. "For God so loved the world, that he gave his only begotten Son, that whosoever believeth in him should not perish, but have everlasting life" (John 3:16).

PARALLEL MINISTRY OF JESUS AND JOHN

During the summer Jesus and John carried on parallel ministries in the land of Judaea where they preached, "The kingdom of God is at hand" and baptized (although Jesus did not personally baptize). John publicly reproved Herod Antipas, the ruler of Peraea and Galilee, for living with his brother's wife; and Herod had John imprisoned in Machaerus. Locate Machaerus on the map in Appendix G. When this happened, Jesus departed to go again into Galilee through Samaria.

RECEPTION AND REJECTION OF CHRIST

The Jews involved in the temple business rejected Him because He interfered in their business, but many did believe on Jesus and came to Him. Nicodemus either at this time or later became a believer (John 19:39).

MEMORY HELPS

The letters FFNJJ are just a memory help. Each letter stands for one of the important events in this period. The first *F* stands for the first Passover. The second *F* stands for the first cleansing of the temple. The *N* stands for new birth and Nicodemus. The first *J* stands for Jesus, and the second *J* stands for John and the parallel ministry he had with Jesus in Judaea. (The two J's are side by side, parallel.) Because of the rhythm, the order should be easy to remember: FFNJJ.

WHAT GOD IS LIKE

His power: Christ revealed it in His miracles (John 2:23).

His knowledge: He foreknew about His death and resurrection (John 2:19-21; 3:14). He knew the hearts of men (John 2:25). He knew He had an appointment with a woman in Samaria (John 4:4).

His love: God gave His most precious gift (John 3:16).

His justice: Judgment on sin has been passed (John 3:18).

His mercy: He sent His Son to save the condemned (John 3:17).

QUESTIONS FOR MEDITATION

1. The Jews often traveled many miles to worship at the Passover. Do you think enough of the Lord to make an effort to regularly attend public worship of Him?
2. Jesus began His ministry with the cleansing of the temple. In I Corinthians 6:19-20, the Christian's body is called the temple of God. Have you allowed the Lord to cleanse your temple that you might minister for Him?
3. The center of this period is the discourse on the new birth. Is it the central truth of your ministry?
4. John the Baptist faithfully proclaimed his message to the rich and poor, the religious leaders, and the very king. It cost him his life. Are you that faithful?
5. There came a time when John realized that his ministry was drawing to a close; but he said, "He [Christ] must increase, but I must decrease." Are you willing for Christ to receive the glory—not only willing, but eager —as John was?

    See Appendixes H and B.

CHAPTER 7

CHRIST IN SAMARIA

FALL OF A.D. 27

KEY WORD: WELL

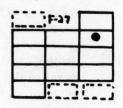

Key Events	Mark	Luke	John
1. Woman at the *well* (Sychar)			4:5-42
2. Nobleman's son made *well* (Jesus at Cana and son at Capernaum)			4:43-54
3. Jesus preaches in the synagogues of Galilee and is *well* received (first Galilean tour, probably alone)	1:14-15	4:14-15	

A SPIRIT-FILLED LIFE

Jesus' life is a perfect example of a life controlled by the Spirit of God. Even as Jesus was led into the wilderness to be tempted, so He was led by the Spirit of God to return to Galilee (Luke 4:14); but "he must needs go through Samaria." A Jew usually avoided Samaria by going up the Jordan Valley, but Jesus stopped at Jacob's well to talk to a woman.

This woman lived in a town called Sychar located between two famous mountains, Mount Ebal and Mount Gerizim. When Joshua brought the people into the land, he divided them into two groups. Half of them stood over against Mount Gerizim and half over against Mount Ebal. Joshua read all the blessings and cursings of the law. As Jesus talked with the woman, she realized that this was no ordinary man, so she asked Him whether He thought the proper place

38

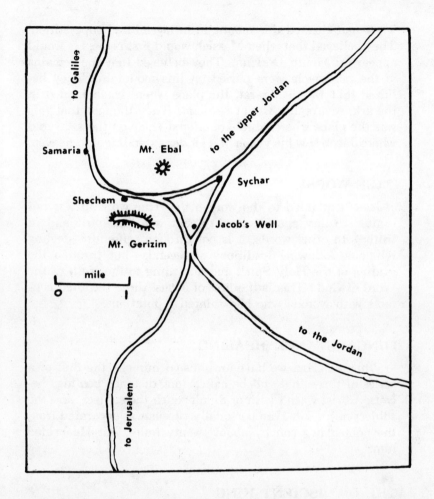

to worship was on Mount Gerizim or in Jerusalem. This was not an idle question.

SAMARITAN HOLY MOUNTAIN

Mount Gerizim was a special place to the Samaritans. They had built a temple there which the Jews had destroyed in 129 B.C. It had stood there for about two hundred years.

They had cloaked this mountain in legend and superstition. They believed that when Messiah would first come, He would appear on Mount Gerizim. They believed that the remains of the tabernacle were buried on this mountain. They believed that Mount Ararat, the place where Noah landed in the ark, was really Mount Gerizim. They thought that this was the place where Abraham offered Isaac on the altar and where Jacob saw his vision of a ladder extending into heaven.

TRUE WORSHIP

Jesus explained to the woman that true worship was not limited to any specific locality, but was "in spirit and in truth." In other words, it is not through self-effort—feeling religious, following traditions or legends—but through the leading of the Holy Spirit and according to the truth of the Word of God. This is the first of Jesus' three recorded contacts with women who had tainted reputations.

LONG-DISTANCE HEALING

While at Cana we have an unusual miracle, the first of a series of three that will be called long-distance healings because Christ wasn't with or didn't touch the subject, and the subject never saw Him personally. Jesus was separated from the nobleman's son by about twenty miles, but He healed him.

THE OMNISCIENT KING

When Jesus talked to the woman at the well, she told Him, "I know that Messias cometh, which is called Christ: when he is come, he will tell us all things." Jesus said unto her, "I that speak unto thee am he" (John 4:25-26). It was prophesied in Isaiah 66:15-18 that Messiah would be omniscient, that He would know all things. Jesus told the woman about her wicked life.

KINGDOM PROCLAIMED ON FIRST GALILEAN TOUR

The third incident recorded in this period is the synagogue preaching ministry that Jesus had in Galilee. Luke 4:15 says, "And he taught in their synagogues, being glorified of all." Jesus preached, "The time is fulfilled, and the kingdom of God is at hand: repent ye, and believe the gospel" (Mark 1:15). Jesus was the King promised to Israel in the Davidic Covenant (II Sam. 7:8-17). He came in this fulfillment as Saviour and King. Many would have followed Him as King but rejected Him as Saviour. This was the first of four Galilean tours that He made. The Bible doesn't tell whether or not He was alone; but the following spring Jesus again called His disciples, so evidently they did not stay with Him continually.

RECEPTION AND REJECTION OF CHRIST

The woman believed that Jesus was the promised Messiah and went back into the city to tell others. The Samaritans asked Jesus to stay in their village, and many believed on Him. The nobleman believed on Christ; the people of Galilee received Him; and "he taught in their synagogues, being glorified of all" (Luke 4:15). The opposition would begin to develop in a few months, starting at Nazareth.

MEMORY HELPS

The key word for this period is WELL. The woman was at the *well*, the nobleman's son was made *well*, and Jesus was *well* received in the Galilean synagogues.

WHAT GOD IS LIKE

His omniscience: He knows all things. Jesus knew even the intimate sordid history of the woman.

His omnipotence: The long-distance healing of the nobleman's son demonstrated the power of God to whom space is no problem (Ps. 139).

41

QUESTIONS FOR MEDITATION

1. Jesus was willing to take the gospel to a woman who was an outcast socially, morally and racially. Are your prejudices preventing you from being used of the Lord?

2. The woman didn't let her sinful past become an excuse to keep her from telling others about Christ. Are you making excuses or making Christ known?

3. The nobleman believed the Lord had the power to heal his son. Are you limiting the Lord's ministry to you or through you, by your unbelief?

CHAPTER 8

REJECTED AT NAZARETH

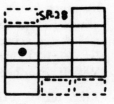

SPRING OF A.D. 28

KEY WORD: BLDG.–

Key Events	Matthew	Mark	Luke
1. B elligerent rejection (first) at Nazareth			4:16-31
Jesus makes His new home at Capernaum	4:13-17		
2. L ot of fishes (Sea of Galilee near Capernaum)			
Call of four disciples	4:18-22	1:16-20	5:1-11
3. D emoniac healed on Sabbath (Capernaum)		1:21-28	4:31-37
Peter's mother-in-law healed (Capernaum)	8:14-17	1:29-34	4:38-41
4. G alilean tour (second) with four disciples	4:23-25	1:35-39	4:42-44
Leper healed, sent to Jerusalem	8:2-4	1:40-45	5:12-16
5. · Roof opened for sick man (Capernaum)	9:1-8	2:1-12	5:17-26
6. ⁻Call of Matthew, and his feast (Capernaum)	9:9-17	2:13-22	5:27-39

Read at least the fullest account of each event.

Find the location of each key event on the map in Appendix G. Study the synagogue in Appendix B.

43

FIRST REJECTION OF THE MESSIAH AT NAZARETH

Up to this time Jesus had been well received in the synagogues of Galilee. He returned to Nazareth and in the synagogue read from the Prophet Isaiah the essence of His program: "The Spirit of the Lord is upon me, because [1] he hath anointed me to preach the gospel to the poor; [2] he hath sent me to heal the brokenhearted, [3] to preach deliverance to the captives, [4] and recovering of sight to the blind, [5] to set at liberty them that are bruised, [6] to preach the acceptable year of the Lord" (Luke 4:18-19; see Isa. 61:1-2). This was a well-known Messianic prophecy. Yet His own people rejected Him and wanted to kill Him.

THE KING PROCEEDS WITH HIS PROGRAM

Even though He was rejected in Nazareth, Jesus began to carry out His program. In the next few weeks He (1) preached the gospel to the poor as He went on His second and third Galilean tours proclaiming the good news that the kingdom of God was at hand, (2) healed the brokenhearted as He restored the dead son to his sorrowing mother, (3) proclaimed deliverance to the captives as He cast out demons, (4) gave sight to the blind, (5) set at liberty them that were bruised as He healed all manner of sickness including leprosy, and (6) preached the acceptable year of the Lord.

A LOT OF FISHES AND THE CALL OF FOUR DISCIPLES

Near His new home in Capernaum on the shore of Galilee, Jesus found Peter, Andrew, James and John. They had spent a fruitless night fishing, but Jesus miraculously provided a multitude of fish. After His resurrection, He performed a similar miracle. The disciples had met Jesus in the fall of 26, but now He told them to follow Him. They were to "catch men." "And . . . they forsook all, and followed him" (Luke 5:10-11).

A DEMON-POSSESSED MAN

At the synagogue in Capernaum Jesus was confronted with the first of many demon-possessed men whom He encountered in His ministry. These demons were evil spirits, whom many Bible students believe to be fallen angels. They entered and controlled human beings, using their voices and controlling their body actions. This demon recognized Jesus as the "Holy One of God," but Jesus rebuked him and commanded him to come out of the man. Jesus didn't want a testimony from a questionable source. This amazed the people because here was a teacher who not only taught with authority but also had power, even over the evil spirits.

Many people have attempted to explain away demon possession as a disease that we know today as epilepsy. The Bible, in Mark 1:24, makes clear the distinction between demon possession and epilepsy.

When Christ reigns in Jerusalem during the millennium, Satan will be bound. The forces of evil will not have the liberty that they now have on the earth. When Jesus cast the demon out of the man in Capernaum, that act foreshadowed the spiritual condition in His kingdom.

PETER'S MOTHER-IN-LAW

Some people teach that Peter was the first Pope, but they say that Popes and priests should not marry. The Scriptures do not say that Peter was a Pope, but they do say that Jesus performed a miracle by raising his mother-in-law from her sickbed and restoring her to strength so that she "rose up and ministered unto them."

Both of these miracles, healing the demon-possessed man and restoring Peter's mother-in-law, were performed on the sabbath. The report of these miracles went out into all the region of Galilee (Mark 1:28). At sundown, as soon as the sabbath was over, they brought many sick people to Him; and He healed every one. This foreshadowed the physical condition of His kingdom and points to the eternal state where the redeemed will have all the curse of sin removed.

KINGDOM PROCLAIMED ON THE SECOND GALILEAN TOUR

On His second Galilean tour Jesus took His four disciples with Him. In the synagogues He preached the gospel of the kingdom and healed all kinds of diseases. His fame continued to spread, and multitudes began to follow Him. They came from Syria, Galilee, Decapolis, Judaea, Jerusalem and beyond Jordan (Peraea).

A LEPER IS HEALED

This is the first mention of Jesus healing a leper. According to tradition the scribes taught that if it was a windless day, you were defiled if you got within six feet of a leper. If it was a windy day, you were not to get within one hundred feet of him or you were ceremonially unclean. But Jesus touched the leper and removed the source of defilement, the disease of leprosy. After he was healed, Jesus gave the leper a special mission to go to the priest in Jerusalem and show himself to him according to the commandments given in the Old Testament (Lev. 14:1-7). This special healing was to be a "testimony unto them" (Mark 1:44). He was, in effect, presenting through the healed leper His credentials as Messiah to the religious leaders of Israel. The leper's special instructions were that he was to say nothing to anyone he met along the way, but he disobeyed the Lord and began to publish it widely so that many people came seeking Him. Jesus couldn't enter openly into a city but had to withdraw to the desert places. The leper's disobedience hindered the Lord's ministry.

Sickness is a symptom of the disease of sin. Although there were many sick people, Jesus left them and withdrew into the desert and prayed. God's plan was to do more than treat the symptom. Jesus was going to provide the cure for the disease of sin.

IS HE GOD?

When Jesus returned to Capernaum, He was teaching in a house crowded with people. Among those present were Pharisees and doctors of the law (rabbis) that were come out of every village of Galilee, Judaea and Jerusalem (Luke 5:17). When a palsied man's friends could not get him to Jesus because of the crowd, they opened the tiles of the roof and let him down into the midst before Jesus. He said unto him, "Thy sins be forgiven thee."

"And the scribes and the Pharisees began to reason, saying, Who is this which speaketh blasphemies? Who can forgive sins, but God alone?" (Luke 5:21). This was the issue— Is Jesus God? Jesus knew their hearts and could read their thoughts so He asked, "Whether is easier, to say, Thy sins be forgiven thee; or to say, Rise up and walk?" (Luke 5:23). Then He commanded the man to take up his bed and go to his house, and he did.

DINNER TABLE EVANGELISM

After Jesus healed the man let through the roof, He left the house, saw Matthew, and called him to be His disciple. Matthew forsook all and followed Jesus. But Matthew was concerned about his friends; he made a feast and invited a multitude of publicans and sinners so that they might meet Jesus.

RECEPTION AND REJECTION OF CHRIST

When Jesus went to Nazareth, His hometown, He was rejected by the people, who even attempted to kill Him. As Jesus ministered at the Capernaum synagogue, the multitudes received Him as a teacher and a healer; but most of them probably didn't receive Him as the Messiah. The leper, the four friends of the palsied man, and Matthew seem to be examples of those who had more than normal spiritual discernment. The scribes and Pharisees, however, were not willing to believe that Jesus was God. Even the evidence He

47

gave as He demonstrated His power to heal, seemed to have no effect upon them.

MEMORY HELPS

The key word for this period is BLDG.-. There is a building connected with each of the events. Jesus' first rejection took place in the *synagogue* in Nazareth. He then made His *home* in Capernaum. When He called His four disciples, they left their *homes* and followed Him. The first demon-possessed man was healed in a *synagogue*. Peter's mother-in-law was healed in Peter's *house*. The second Galilean tour was primarily a *synagogue* ministry. The leper was sent to the priest in Jerusalem who would be at the *temple*. The man who was palsied was let through a hole in the roof of a *house*. Then Matthew prepared a feast in his *house*.

The first letters in the first four key events on the chart spell out the abbreviation BLDG. Notice that most of these events took place in Capernaum. The period represents the hole in the roof, and the dash represents Matthew's table.

WHAT GOD IS LIKE

His power: Jesus demonstrated His power as He passed through the midst of the angry crowd at Nazareth when they desired to kill Him. It was also displayed over nature as He brought the multitude of fishes to the exact spot where the fishermen could lower their nets and catch them, even though these experienced fishermen didn't believe that there was anything there. It was displayed over the forces of evil as He cast out demons. Jesus displayed His power over disease, including leprosy.

His compassion: He stretched forth His hand and healed the leper.

His knowledge: He understood the reasonings of the hearts of the scribes and the Pharisees.

His forgiveness: Jesus forgave the palsied man's sins.

JESUS THE PERFECT MAN

The Scriptures record that it was Jesus' custom to attend the synagogue. A man of God should be regular in worship. It is often hard to separate the divine characteristics of Christ and His characteristics as the perfect Man. This is as it should be. Man was created in the image of God, and at his best (in Christ) should be godlike, reflecting the glory of God.

QUESTIONS FOR MEDITATION

1. The people of Nazareth couldn't believe that Jesus was the Messiah because He had lived among them. Do you have the proper respect for the Christian leaders that the Lord has put in your church?
2. The four fisherman disciples left their relatives, their businesses and their possessions and followed Jesus. Have you let any of these things stand between you and serving the Lord?
3. Jesus didn't allow the demon to testify concerning Him. A testimony from an evil source would not help but would hinder His ministry. Is your testimony before the world a help or a hindrance for Christ?
4. The leper was without doubt very happy about his healing. Perhaps he reasoned to himself and decided that everyone should know about Jesus. Have you allowed your reasoning or ideas to cause you to disobey the Lord's directions for your life?
5. Jesus and His disciples were criticized by the scribes and Pharisees for associating with the publicans and sinners. They misunderstood Jesus' motive. Have you been unfair in your criticism of others? Because of your fear of being criticized, have you avoided contact with unsaved acquaintances?

49

CHAPTER 9

THE GREAT DECISION

SUMMER OF A.D. 28

KEY WORD: MAN

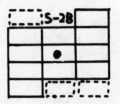

Key Events	Matthew	Mark	Luke	John
1. Impotent man at the pool (Jerusalem)				5:1-47
Disciples pluck grain (Galilee?)	12:1-8	2:23-28	6:1-5	
Man with withered hand (Capernaum)	12:9-21	3:1-12	6:6-11	
2. Jesus chooses twelve apostles (Galilee)		3:13-19	6:12-16	
Sermon on the Mount (Horns of Hattin)	5:1—8:1		6:17-49	
Centurion's servant healed (Capernaum)	8:5-13		7:1-10	
3. Widow's son raised at Nain			7:11-17	
Men inquire for John the Baptist (Galilee)	11:2-30		7:18-35	
First anointing of Jesus' feet (Capernaum)			7:36-50	
4. Tour of Galilee with the twelve apostles (third)			8:1-3	
Demon-possessed, blind, dumb man healed (Capernaum?)				
Jews say it is by Beelzebub, demand a sign	12:22-45	3:20-30		
Friends and family think He is crazy	12:46-50	3:21, 31-35	8:19-21	

50

Read at least the fullest account of each event.

THE MIDDLE OF CHRIST'S EARTHLY MINISTRY

The summer of 28 is the middle period in the earthly ministry of Christ. Many important things happened during this period. It began with Christ attending a feast in Jerusalem, probably the Passover.

A SIGN-MIRACLE DEMONSTRATING HIS DEITY

Jesus told the man at the pool, who had been sick for thirty-eight years, to take up his bed and walk; but the Jews, instead of recognizing that Jesus was God, became very angry because Jesus and the man were not keeping the Sabbath in the way they felt was proper. The Sabbath became a big issue between the Jews and Jesus (see Appendix L on the Sabbath). Another accusation that comes from this passage (John 5:1-18) was that Jesus made Himself equal with God, or, in other words, was God. The Jews considered this blasphemy.

CHRIST'S PROOFS OF DEITY

In His humanity as the God-man, Jesus was dependent on the Father's will; and He didn't act independently of Him. But Jesus not only claimed to be God; He gave the following proofs to support this claim (John 5:19-30):

1. He and the Father are equal in works. He can do what the Father can.

2. He and the Father have power of life.

3. The Father has the power to judge, but He has committed all judgment unto the Son (Rev. 20:11).

4. He and the Father are equal in honor; you can't honor the Father and reject the Son.

5. He and the Father have the power of resurrection.

WITNESSES TO CHRIST'S DEITY

Jesus then pointed out five witnesses that had testified that what He had said was true (John 5:30-37):

1. John the Baptist
2. The works of Jesus
3. The Father—His voice was heard at Jesus' baptism.
4. The Scriptures
5. Moses—This is a reference particularly to the writ-ings of Moses, the first five books of the Bible.

THE SECOND SABBATH CONTROVERSY

As Jesus and His disciples returned to Galilee, they were hungry. So they plucked grain and ate it. The Pharisees became very angry, but Jesus defended their conduct by reminding them (1) that when David was hungry, he ate the shewbread which it was not lawful for him to eat—a work of necessity; (2) that the priests worked on the Sabbath in the temple—a work of worship; and (3) that the Sabbath was made for man and not man for the Sabbath (Mark 2:27-28). He then made a very startling statement: "In this place is one [Messiah] greater than the temple" (Matt. 12:6). "For the Son of man is Lord even of the sabbath day" (Matt. 12:8).

THIRD SABBATH CONTROVERSY

After returning to Galilee, Jesus entered into a synagogue and taught. Among the audience were scribes and Pharisees and a man with a withered hand. It appears that perhaps the Pharisees brought the man because the Scriptures say that they watched Jesus to see if they could accuse Him. Jesus didn't touch the man but just told him to stretch forth his hand, and it was healed. This made them very angry; and they took counsel with the Herodians to find a way they could destroy Him (Matt. 12:14). The Herodians were a political party with which the Pharisees usually did not associate (see Appendixes R and Z).

THE KING CHOOSES TWELVE APOSTLES

After a night of prayer, Jesus chose twelve apostles from among His many followers, or disciples. He chose them that they might be with Him and that He might send them forth to preach the kingdom of God, cast out demons, heal the sick and raise the dead (Matt. 10:7-8; Mark 3:14-15; Luke 9:1-2). These twelve continued with Him for almost two years. Notice that the twelve apostles were not with Jesus for three and a half years as is commonly taught.

SERMON ON THE MOUNT

Jesus went up on a nearby mountain. It was probably the Horns of Hattin, a small mountain only twelve hundred feet high with two points. Finding a level spot, He gave the famous discourse the Sermon on the Mount. Many books have been written on this sermon, and there are many different interpretations as to its exact purpose and meaning. The Beatitudes have been memorized by many through the ages. Some Bible scholars have pointed out that the Beatitudes are really summaries of Old Testament promises that Jesus will fulfill when He rules as the promised King of Israel during His millennial kingdom.

The people realized that Jesus' interpretation of the Scriptures, was different from that of the scribes. They quoted from other rabbis' and scribes' opinions; Jesus spoke with authority. He assured them that He did not come to destroy the Law and the Prophets but to fulfill them (Matt. 5:17).

THE STANDARD OF RIGHTEOUSNESS FOR THE KINGDOM

In the Sermon on the Mount, Jesus stated the standard of righteousness that was required for the kingdom. "Except your righteousness shall exceed the righteousness of the scribes and Pharisees, ye shall in no case enter into the kingdom of heaven" (Matt. 5:20). The Pharisees thought that they alone, because of their knowledge of the law and the traditions, had a chance of being accepted by God. They considered the common people cursed because they knew not the law.

In contrast to what the scribes taught, Jesus seemed to be

teaching in Matthew 5:21-48 that outward conformity is not enough, but inward conformity to the law of God is needed to enter His kingdom. In Matthew 6 He said that a person can appear to be practicing righteous acts such as almsgiving, prayer and fasting and still be doing it in a hypocritical manner. In Matthew 6:19-34 Jesus taught that a person truly devoted to God won't have to worry about material things; God will meet His needs.

The Pharisees were very self-righteous, but Jesus warned them in Matthew 7 to beware of judging others because they will be judged with the same judgment they put on others. Then He illustrated His teaching with several very pointed parables. On the human level, the standard of righteousness Christ required is impossible. The new birth is a necessity (John 3:3) not only for His kingdom but also for eternal salvation.

GOD'S STANDARD OF RIGHTEOUSNESS

As Jesus ministered on earth and revealed what God is like, the people became aware that they needed more than just a king. They also needed a Saviour. In the spring of 28 after Jesus had produced the miraculous draught of fishes, Simon Peter said, "Depart from me; for I am a sinful man, O Lord" (Luke 5:8). A Saviour from sin was a great stumbling block for the scribes and the Pharisees. They did not want to acknowledge that their righteousness was not acceptable to God. Jesus taught that the righteousness that will be acceptable in the kingdom is not an outward righteousness of tradition but an inward righteousness of the heart.

When Jesus taught His disciples to pray, one of the requests was "Thy kingdom come." They were also told, "Seek ye first the kingdom of God, and his righteousness; and all these things shall be added unto you" (Matt. 6:33). They entered the kingdom by receiving the King, and He in turn provided them with the required righteousness. This was not to be just an outward lip service but a sincerity that changed lives (Matt. 7:21).

54

THE SECOND LONG-DISTANCE HEALING

A centurion (a Roman army officer who had charge of one hundred soldiers) sent to Jesus and asked Him to heal one of his servants; and Jesus did heal him. Neither the sick man nor the centurion saw or had any personal contact with Christ. Jesus marveled at the faith of the centurion and declared, "Many [Gentiles] shall come from the east and west, and shall sit down with Abraham, and Isaac, and Jacob, in the kingdom of heaven. But the children of the kingdom shall be cast out into outer darkness: there shall be weeping and gnashing of teeth" (Matt. 8:11-12; see Ps. 107:3; Isa. 49:12). This passage teaches several things about the kingdom:

1. The Gentiles will have a place in it.
2. The Old Testament saints to whom the kingdom was promised will be resurrected and will share in the kingdom.
3. The sons of the kingdom (Jews who reject the King) will be cast out into outer darkness. They could have participated in the kingdom because of the promise, or covenant, that God made with Israel, but they rejected the King.

WIDOW'S SON RESTORED TO LIFE

Jesus next performed the most startling miracle of His ministry up to that time. He raised the dead. This death was a very sad occasion. A family was facing extinction. A widow had lost her only son. There was no one to carry on the family name. But as this sad procession moved toward the cemetery, carrying the body of the young man, they met Jesus the Prince of Life; and He restored the young man to life.

This little scene is representative of the condition of the human race. Man has sinned and rebelled against God and is under the curse of death. He is traveling down the sorrowful road of time without hope and with only righteous judgment at the end. But God in His great love has chosen to intervene and provide a way of escape. Jesus came into the

55

world and took our sins upon Himself and paid the penalty
for them (I Peter 2:24). He has conquered death, and He
offers life unto all who believe on Him.

In the kingdom it will be unusual for a young man to die.
"And I will rejoice in Jerusalem, and joy in my people: and
the voice of weeping shall be no more heard in her, nor the
voice of crying. There shall be no more thence an infant
of days, nor an old man that hath not filled his days: for
the child shall die an hundred years old" (Isa. 65:19-20). By
this restoration from the dead, the King brought this kingdom condition to the city of Nain.

JOHN THE BAPTIST'S MEN QUESTION JESUS

John the Baptist had been in jail about a year when he
began to wonder whether Jesus really was the Messiah. He
sent some of his friends to ask.

Jesus performed a special series of miracles that day and
told them to go back and tell John "how that the blind see,
the lame walk, the lepers are cleansed, the deaf hear, the
dead are raised, to the poor the gospel is preached" (Luke
7:22). These were the credentials of the Messiah as prophesied in the Old Testament (see Isa. 29:18-19; 35:5-6; 61:1).

DINNER TABLE EVANGELISM #2

An unbelieving Pharisee wanted Jesus to eat with Him.
The Pharisee was very critical of Jesus when a woman with
an immoral reputation came in and anointed His feet. The
Pharisee couldn't believe that Jesus was any more than a
man. He felt that if Jesus were really a prophet or the
Messiah, He wouldn't let this woman even touch Him. According to the Pharisees' interpretation of the law this would
make a man ceremonially unclean. Because of her faith,
Jesus told the woman that her sins were forgiven. Once
again the Pharisees were face to face with this issue: Who
can forgive sins but God? The Pharisees present at the
dinner wouldn't receive Jesus as God, especially when He

56

didn't act according to their concept of the way a righteous person should act.

KINGDOM PROCLAIMED ON THIRD GALILEAN TOUR

For the third time Jesus went through the villages and cities, but this time He took with Him His twelve disciples. They preached the good news of the kingdom of God (Luke 8:1-2). Jesus was preparing them for a future ministry, for the following spring He would send them out two by two over Galilee again.

THE BIG DECISION: WHO IS JESUS?

The ministry of Jesus to this point had caused such a stir that people began to make personal decisions. Mark 3:19-21 records that Jesus' friends, probably from Nazareth, came to Him and were going to take Him by force because they felt He was beside Himself. In Greek the words "beside himself" actually mean "insane." Even Jesus' mother and brethren didn't understand His ministry and wanted to persuade Him to go home with them.

A demon-possessed blind and dumb man was healed by Jesus. The scribes and the Pharisees couldn't deny that the man was healed; but they didn't want to attribute this power to Jesus as God or even as an agent for God. They said instead that He cast out demons by the power of Beelzebub, the prince of demons. Jesus told them (1) that this was a foolish answer. Was Satan casting out Satan? If he was, he was divided against himself. Jesus stated (2) that some of the scribes also cast out demons at various times; and He asked, "By whom do your sons cast them out?" Then He summarized His argument by saying (3) that if He cast out demons by the Spirit of God, then the kingdom of God had come unto them.

The scribes and the Pharisees still would not admit that they were wrong, and they asked Jesus for another sign. He told them that they wouldn't receive any other sign except the sign of Jonah. He was referring to His death, burial and resurrection. After this rejection by the religious leaders of Israel, the whole character of Jesus' ministry changed. He continued, however, to present Himself as the King until He was finally crucified with the proclamation on the cross: "Jesus of Nazareth, King of the Jews."

RECEPTION AND REJECTION OF CHRIST

During this period we begin to see people fall into three categories. First, there were those who thought Jesus was a LIAR, an impostor, a blasphemer, or an evil worker. This included most of the religious leaders. They didn't like the way that Jesus kept the sabbath nor His interpretation of the law. The second group thought that Jesus was a LUNA-TIC. This included some of His friends and perhaps some of His own family. The third group recognized that Jesus was the LORD. This included many common people, the centurion, and many publicans and harlots.

LIKE SPOILED CHILDREN

Jesus compared those who were rejecting Him to spoiled children. "They are like unto children sitting in the market-place, and calling to one another, and saying, We have piped unto you, and ye have not danced; we have mourned to you, and ye have not wept" (see Luke 7:27-35). Jesus did not play their "games" with them. Because He did not come and keep all the Jewish traditions nor act according to their idea of the Messiah, they rejected Him.

REJECTION WILL BRING JUDGMENT

Jesus offered Himself as Messiah on three tours of Galilee and preached the kingdom of God also in Samaria and Judaea, but they did not repent. "Woe unto thee, Chorazin! woe unto thee, Bethsaida! for if the mighty works, which were done in you, had been done in Tyre and Sidon, they would have repented long ago in sackcloth and ashes" (Matt. 11:20-24; see Luke 13:34).

The Bible records that doubt comes even to great leaders. Jesus commended John the Baptist very highly, but after a year in jail John's faith began to waver. There seem to have been multitudes following Jesus who were not really aware of the real issue. Even though the religious rulers were turning from Him, multitudes continued to follow Him. In Matthew 12:23-24 they asked the question "Is not this the son of David?" By this they were asking, "Is this the promised Messiah?" However, the construction in the original Greek is so worded as to indicate that they expected a negative answer: "No, this is not the Messiah."

MEMORY HELPS

The key word for this period is MAN. The main events are grouped in groups of three. It will be easier to remember them in little clusters. The travels can be traced on a map in four loops. If a peg were driven in a map at Capernaum and a rope were coiled on it, it would look like the journeys of Jesus during this period.

In the first big loop we have the journey down to Jerusalem where Jesus healed the *man at the pool*. On the way back to Galilee, Jesus' disciples plucked grain and were criticized by the Jews. Jesus replied that the *Sabbath was made for man* and not man for the Sabbath. When He arrived in a synagogue in Capernaum, He healed a *man with a withered hand*.

The second loop includes Jesus' choosing twelve apostles, or *twelve men*. Jesus gave the Sermon on the Mount to *His twelve men* (as well as to a multitude of disciples). This mountain has twin peaks and is shaped like the letter *M*. Then Jesus healed the centurion's servant. This was back in Capernaum and can be remembered by the phrase "Jesus heals a *big man's man*."

The events in the third loop include the raising of the widow's son. This can be remembered because he was the

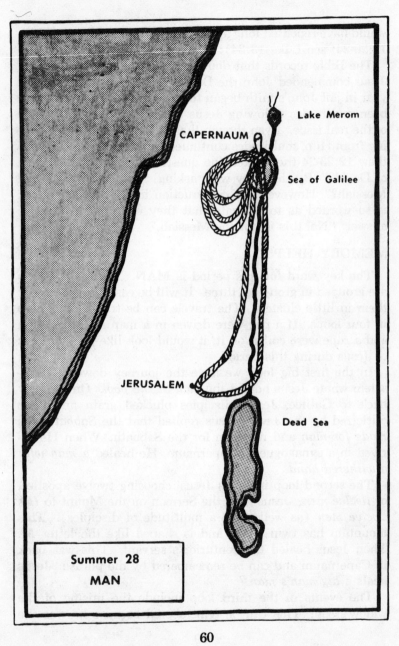

Lake Merom

CAPERNAUM

Sea of Galilee

JERUSALEM

Dead Sea

Summer 28
MAN

last man in the family. Back in Capernaum at the anointing of Jesus' feet, the Pharisee considered Jesus *only a man* because He let the woman touch Him.

The fourth loop includes the third tour of Galilee with the twelve. After they had returned to Capernaum, He healed the demon-possessed, blind, dumb man (*DBD man*). This key figure is the only person mentioned who was demon-possessed as well as blind and dumb.

WHAT GOD IS LIKE

His power: Jesus continued to heal the sick, cast out demons, and raise the dead.

His omniscience: His knowledge of all things was revealed as He discerned the thoughts and intents of the hearts of men.

His righteousness: Jesus revealed His righteousness in His daily work and attitude toward life as contrasted with the hypocrisy of the Pharisees.

His grace and compassion: He restored the widow's son to life. The Bible doesn't tell any more about this widow and her son; but since God is a God of grace who does "exceeding abundantly above all that we ask or think" (Eph. 3:20), He gave the widow back her son, and probably also gave her a half-dozen healthy grandsons to rejoice over in the years that followed.

His anger: He showed His anger at the Pharisees who tried to find something of which they could accuse Him, but Christ was *grieved* because of the hardness of their hearts (Mark 3:5).

His impartiality: He evangelized all levels of society (Matt. 11:19).

His forgiveness: He forgave the sins of the woman who anointed His feet (Luke 7:48-49).

His wisdom: He answered the false charge of the Pharisees (Matt. 12:22-29).

61

JESUS THE PERFECT MAN

Jesus was a worker (John 5:17; 9:4), but it wasn't busy-work nor work by Himself that was independent of the Father (John 5:19). Independent action apart from the will of God is sin. Just because someone says, "This is God's work that I'm doing" doesn't necessarily mean that it is. It may be just busywork, a pet project, or something done for personal profit. Jesus said that God will tell some people who will claim that they have preached, fought evil, and done wonderful works in His name, "I never knew you: depart from me, ye that work iniquity" (Matt. 7:22-23). The key is doing the will of the Father (Matt. 7:21).

Jesus as the perfect Man came to fulfill the law, God's perfect standard of conduct (Matt. 5:17). He wasn't proud but was "meek and lowly in heart" (Matt. 11:29).

QUESTIONS FOR MEDITATION

1. Luke 6:7 says that the scribes and Pharisees went to the synagogue so they could find a reason to accuse Jesus. What is your attitude when you go to church? Do you go to find fault?
2. Jesus marveled at the faith of the centurion. Is your faith something that honors Christ? Or is your thinking so clouded with doubt that it is a reproach?
3. The woman who anointed Jesus' feet was very thankful for all He had done for her. Would your attitude toward Him be like the woman's or like the Pharisee's?
4. Is your "Christian" service really Christian because the Lord has told you to do it, or is it busywork? Is it a pet project of your own, something you do to get personal profit?

See Appendix L.

CHAPTER 10

PARABLES BY THE SEA

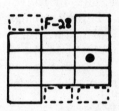

FALL OF A.D. 28

KEY WORD: SEA

Key Events	Matthew	Mark	Luke
1. Kingdom of heaven parables by the sea (Capernaum)	13:1-53	4:1-34	8:4-18
2. Stilling the tempest on the sea	8:18, 23-27	4:35-41	8:22-25
3. Demoniac in graveyard, swine into the sea (Gadarenes)	8:28-34	5:1-20	8:26-39
4. Crossing back over the sea to Capernaum, four miracles: Jairus' daughter raised Woman touches Christ's garment Two blind men and dumb demoniac healed	9:18-26 9:27-34	5:21-43	8:40-56

Read at least the fullest account of every event.

The events of this period all occur around the Sea of Galilee. Study the map in Appendix G and locate each of the key events on it.

KINGDOM OF HEAVEN PARABLES BY THE SEA

After the religious rulers rejected Jesus as King and Messiah and attributed His miracles to evil powers, the character of His ministry changed. He had been teaching in many of the synagogues, but much of His ministry from this point on was carried on outdoors. Jesus had used parables in His

63

ministry before, but now He gave a great series of parables. When His disciples wanted to know why He did this, He gave them three reasons for using parables at this time: (1) to reveal truth, (2) to hide truth, and (3) to fulfill prophecy (Matt. 13:10-16; Isa. 6:9-10).

Parables or figures of speech can very effectively illustrate a principle or a doctrine; but if a person does not accept or understand the doctrine or teaching, the parable will hide the truth because the person gets lost in the details of the story.

WARNING!

Remember that parables are figures of speech. They were given to explain doctrine. Do not try to develop doctrines or teachings from a figure of speech, or you may fall into error. Jesus interpreted part of these parables for His disciples. Follow His interpretation. Don't try to make them teach too much.

THE WORD MYSTERY

In classical Greek the word *mystery* was used to describe certain religious ceremonies or rites practiced by secret societies. Only the initiated could know them. The word mystery as used in the New Testament does not mean something that is mysterious or hard to understand, but it refers to unrevealed truth that can only be known by revelation. Paul explained his usage of the word mystery in Romans 16:25-26. Jesus gave His explanation in Matthew 13:35: "I will open my mouth in parables; I will utter things which have been kept secret from the foundation of the world."

Many books have been written and many sermons have been preached on the kingdom of heaven parables. Generally speaking, they can be divided into three approaches:

1. The first group emphasizes the spiritual and moral values that the parables can be used to illustrate. They usually make no distinction between the church and the kingdom. They consider that the promises of the kingdom

are fulfilled in a spiritual kingdom represented by the church, and consequently the church inherits the kingdom promises given in the Old Testament to Israel. They assume that the church is going to be triumphant and convert the world. This, of course, is in direct contrast to many definite statements in the New Testament (II Tim. 3).

2. The second group teaches that the parables reveal the character and progress of the present dispensation. They teach a "mystery form" of the kingdom for this age. The kingdom includes all Christendom—all those who profess to be Christians. In their teaching, they emphasize the strict interpretation of types: If an object is used in the Bible in one way, it is never used in another; or if an object means one thing in one parable, it will mean the same thing in the next parable. In some cases this appears to be true. In others it will conflict with the plain teaching of the parable or its interpretation as given in the Scriptures. For example, in the first parable of the sower Jesus said that the seed is the word of the kingdom. In the parable of the wheat and the tares He stated, "The good seed are the children of the kingdom." The Scripture also describes Satan as a "roaring lion," and Jesus as the "lion of the tribe of Judah." The parables may be used to teach many valid Bible truths. The great danger is that they confuse the Bible student, and the allegorizing may cause him to miss the simple primary meaning of the parable. There is a similarity between this system's interpretation of the first four parables given in Matthew 13 and some events of early church history; but the church was not known at the time these parables were given.

3. The third group teaches that the parables are primarily related to the nation of Israel and its reception and rejection of the kingdom. In the parables, the Jewish expression "kingdom of heaven" used in Matthew is considered to mean the same as the expression used by Mark and Luke, "kingdom of God." In the parables they are both limited as to time, sphere and inhabitants. The kingdom will go through three stages: (1) The kingdom was given to Jesus Christ,

the Son of David. (2) John the Baptist, Jesus, and His disciples announced that the kingdom of God was at hand, and they invited the people to enter in. (3) Jesus Christ will rule and reign in a literal kingdom in fulfillment of the Davidic Covenant. Because of His rejection by Israel, Jesus revealed for the first time that there was going to be a delay between the time the kingdom was first offered and the time it would be literally set up on the earth. Jesus gives other parables and teachings with added details concerning the kingdom later.

While many applications have been made of the kingdom of heaven parables, their primary application is to the nation of Israel. They cover a span of time from the rejection of Christ by Israel to the reception of Christ by Israel at His second coming. This same approximate time period is covered in the letters to the seven churches in Revelation 2 and 3. The parables are about Israel and the kingdom; the letters are to the churches. Do not confuse them. There is a central teaching to each parable. Don't try to make them teach too much.

To distinguish between these three approaches to the interpretation of the parables, we will use the terms "spiritual kingdom" for the first, "mystery kingdom" for the second, and "delayed kingdom" for the third.

INTERPRETATION OF THE PARABLES

The Lord Himself interpreted the parable of the sower, so there is more agreement on this than on the other parables. Only those who approach it from the "delayed kingdom" viewpoint emphasize that the Word that was sown was the "word of the kingdom" (Matt. 13:19). Jesus asked the disciples, "Know ye not this parable? and then how will ye know all parables?" (Mark 4:13). The disciples had just returned with Jesus from His third tour of Galilee. They had proclaimed the word of the kingdom: Jesus, the Son of

David, was present, and the kingdom of heaven was at hand. The disciples had personally seen the response that this preaching had received from the common people. More recently they had seen the rejection of Christ by the religious rulers. The rulers attributed His miracles to evil power.

Jesus gave and interpreted the parable of the sower and so explained to them that the King and the kingdom of God would be received by only a minority of the people. A very normal question would have come to their minds: *How will You set up Your kingdom, Lord? Will You call the armies of heaven?* To answer this unasked question, Jesus gave another parable, recorded only in the book of Mark, about the growth of the seed (Mark 4:26-29). Most commentators ignore this parable. There will be a period of time between the sowing of the seed and the harvest. The seed, "the word of the kingdom," was planted by John the Baptist, Jesus, and His disciples. It did not bring forth an immediate response nor the literal kingdom. There are several parallels between the maturing of the seed and the later development of the kingdom. From outward appearance, when a seed is placed in the ground, it is hidden from sight and may be dead. After a week or two, depending upon the kind of seed, it will germinate and break through the soil, gradually developing until it is ripe.

The word that the kingdom of God was at hand was planted in Israel. There was little response, and finally the nation crucified their King. From outward appearance it looked as though there was no hope for the kingdom. It was dead. But after a period of time it will spring forth and develop into a mighty kingdom that controls the earth. While this is true, it is very unreasonable to believe that the disciples understood this. The simple teaching of the parable is that the word of the kingdom was proclaimed, there will be a period of time before there is any response, but it will grow to maturity as prophesied.

THE PARABLE OF THE TARES

The Lord also interpreted the parable of the tares. He explained that He Himself is the sower. The good seeds are the sons of the kingdom, and the tares are the sons of the evil one (Matt. 23:33). Those who teach a "spiritual kingdom" and the "mystery kingdom" interpret this parable to describe the conflict between true believers and false believers in the church age. While it is true that such a conflict exists, those who interpret from a "delayed kingdom" approach feel that the words of the Lord refer to the kingdom, with its primary application perhaps being near the end of the present age.

Those who interpret from a "spiritual kingdom" viewpoint usually say that the judgment is the great last judgment day. The other two interpret it as being a judgment before the kingdom is set up. Jesus revealed more details about this judgment in Matthew 25:31-46.

PARABLES OF THE MUSTARD SEED AND THE LEAVEN

Though short, these two parables have occasioned much controversy regarding their meaning. The "spiritual kingdom" teaching is that the mustard seed and the leaven represent the gospel, which is introduced into the world and grows until the world is converted. The mustard seed gives a view of its outward growth; the leaven, of its inner silent growth.

The "mystery kingdom" interpretation, in direct contrast to this, interprets the mustard seed as the outward form of Christendom. It includes all professors, whether true believers or false; and because of its apostasy, or departure from the faith, its shelters the birds (unbelievers) in its branches.

Leaven represents false doctrine, especially concerning Christ. It is introduced by a woman who represents a false religious system. This is the inner contamination of the church, or Christendom. The Bible does teach that there will be a departure from the faith in the professing church; it does *not* teach that the church will convert the world. Much of the strength of the argument for this interpretation comes from the idea that leaven is used in the Bible only in an evil sense. It is claimed that figures are only used symbolically one way in the Bible. This, however, is not true. Many figures are used to represent both good and evil. For example, a tree is used both ways in Psalm 1, Daniel 4, Romans 11, and in the parable of the mustard seed. Adam is used both as a' type of evil and as a type of Christ. As mentioned previously, Satan and Christ are both described as a lion. In the parable of the tares, Jesus said that He was the man; but it will bring nothing but contradiction if you try to substitute Christ in each of these parables where the word *man* occurs. Seed is used in different ways: the word of the kingdom, the children of the kingdom, the children of the evil one and, in this parable, as a mustard seed. In other illustrations Jesus used a mustard seed as He explained the power of faith to His disciples. Surely, following this same line of reasoning, a mustard seed would not be associated with something good, such as faith, then used in this parable to represent something evil.

The "delayed kingdom" interpretation would be that the announcement of the kingdom began very small with one man, John the Baptist (Luke 16:16), and later grew into the millennial kingdom of Christ. It continues the teaching of the little parable of the seed: It is planted, and later grows up greater than all of the herbs. This is not speaking of an abnormal growth for this plant but of something with which the disciples were undoubtedly familiar. Parables were taken from the most common events of everyday life. When Jesus gave the parable of the leaven, He had in view the whole process of a housewife making bread for her family. It is not necessary to make the woman represent a false religion. The Bible does this in Revelation 17, but in Revelation 12 we have a woman representing the nation of Israel.

69

While leaven was not to be in most of the offerings, it was present in the two loaves offered at the Feast of Pentecost (Lev. 23:17). The Israelites were not forbidden to use leaven except during the Feast of Unleavened Bread. The Bible does speak of the leaven of the Pharisees, Sadducees, and Herodians; and Paul questioned the church at Corinth, "Know ye not that a little leaven leaveneth the whole lump?" (I Cor. 5:6). It would seem that the reason leaven was used as an illustration is because of the way it works: silently and secretly until all is leavened. If you adopt the doctrine of the Herodians (compromise), the Pharisees (hypocrisy), or the Sadducees (unbelief in the supernatural), it will slowly affect every area of your life: your business relations, your family relations, your prayer life, your worship and your Bible study. Your very goals in life will be changed and perverted. It would not be an instant change, but a gradual one.

If you make this parable of the leaven teach that all Christendom will be perverted, you make it teach too much. What about the true believers? Yet the parable says "till it was all leavened." Also you must change what Jesus said. He said the kingdom of heaven is "like unto leaven" (Matt. 13:33), and not like "meal" in which a woman hid leaven.

The basic teaching of these two parables is that the word of the kingdom is given; then, after a period of time, the mighty kingdom of Christ is established on the earth.

THE PARABLES OF THE HID TREASURE AND THE PEARL OF GREAT PRICE

The "mystery kingdom" interpretation of the first parable is that Israel is the treasure, hidden in the field of the world, which Christ found and hid again among the nations. He bought it with His death on Calvary. In the parable of the pearl of great price, Christ is the merchant seeking goodly pearls; and the great pearl represents the church. Again He bought it with His death on Calvary. It is true that Israel

70

was dispersed throughout the world when Jerusalem was destroyed in A.D. 70, and that the formation of the church can be compared to the formation of a pearl in an oyster as layer upon layer of secretion is gathered about the particle of sand. The church, however, was still unknown. Christ mentioned it briefly for the first time about eight months later. It would be more appropriate, if this referred to the church, to say that Christ came seeking grains of sand or sinners rather than goodly pearls (Luke 19:10).

The "spiritual kingdom" and "delayed kingdom" interpreters usually interpret these parables as describing the response of two kinds of individuals. The first one unexpectedly heard the word of the kingdom and realized that it was a great treasure. The second was seeking pearls (Matt. 6:33); and when he heard the word of the kingdom, he recognized it as valuable. Both joyfully sold all because they realized the value of the kingdom. This value is hid from those who do not believe (II Cor. 4:4). The two men illustrate the true nature of discipleship (Matt. 16:24).

THE PARABLE OF THE NET

The parable of the net is recognized by all three groups of interpreters as pointing toward a judgment. Those who believe the kingdom is a spiritual kingdom usually also believe in a single judgment and interpret this as describing that judgment. The "mystery kingdom" and "delayed kingdom" interpreters both interpret this parable as referring to the judgment at the end of the tribulation period that will precede the millennial kingdom.

THE PARABLE OF THE HOUSEHOLDER

This parable is ignored by many commentators. Those who interpret the "mystery kingdom" usually teach that a scribe will interpret the last half of the kingdom parables by the first half. A more reasonable interpretation is that a scribe, who is a disciple of the kingdom of heaven and a student of the Scriptures, will bring from these Old Testament scrip-

71

tures both old things or prophecies concerning the kingdom and new things now revealed through these parables. The new things now revealed will supplement the Old Testament prophecies.

SUMMARY

Let us summarize the central truth of each of these parables:

The parable of the sower gives the response as the "word of the kingdom" was preached. Even though there is little response at first, the parable of the seed teaches that it takes time for the seed to grow, but it will grow to maturity (Mark 4:26-29).

The parable of the tares shows the activity of the enemy in this age and the promised judgment at harvesttime (Matt. 13:30).

The parables of the mustard seed and leaven indicate that although the kingdom response is slow at first, after a time it will be very great even as it was prophesied in the Old Testament. At first the majority were rejecting the King and His kingdom, but there was some response.

The parables of the hid treasure and the pearl of great price teach the great value a person puts on the kingdom when he responds to it and really understands it. The man who found the hid treasure represents that person who unexpectedly comes upon the good news of the kingdom of heaven. The merchant man represents those like Anna (Luke 2:36-38) who were expectantly waiting for the Messiah.

The parable of the net revealed that a judgment will come at the end of the world ("consummation of the age" in Greek). Jesus later gave more details about this judgment in the Olivet Discourse.

Those who teach a "mystery kingdom" are using the parables to illustrate Bible truth, and their allegorizing of the parables is often very interesting. The author feels that the greatest problem with this interpretation is that it obscures the primary teaching of Christ that there was going to be a delay from the time of the announcement that the kingdom was at hand until the time it actually would be set up. This preparation of His disciples was necessary before He could teach them about His rejection, death and resurrection; about calling out and forming the church; and about His second coming.

MAN AND THE KINGDOM

Man can pray for the coming of the kingdom (Matt. 6:10); look for it (Luke 23:51); seek it (Matt. 6:33); preach it (Matt. 10:7); persuade others about it (Acts 19:8); suffer for it (II Thess. 1:5); receive it (Mark 10:15); inherit it (Matt. 25:34); reject or refuse it (Matt. 23:13). But none can destroy it (Matt. 16:18).

STILLING THE TEMPEST ON THE SEA

Jesus and His disciples got into a boat to cross to the other side of the Sea of Galilee. A great storm arose; they became frightened and awakened Jesus. They were afraid they were going to perish—yet the very One who had raised the widow's son from the dead a short time before this was in the boat with them. When He exercised His power over the sea and calmed the storm, they were amazed and marveled that the winds and the sea would obey Him.

DEMON-POSSESSED MEN IN THE GRAVEYARD

Jesus and His disciples saw a fearsome sight when they reached the other side. Two wild demon-possessed men had been terrorizing the vicinity. One had unusual strength and could break the chains that bound him. The demons caused him to do unnatural things. He lived in the graveyard and ran around naked. When Jesus talked to the demons and asked them their name, they said it was Legion. A Roman legion was composed of six thousand men.

Some interesting information comes from this episode:

1. The demons know what their final destination is—the lake of fire (Matt. 8:29; 25:41).

2. More than one demon can possess a man; in this case there were many.

3. They can cause the possessed person to have abnormal strength.

4. They often cause the possessed person to do evil and unnatural things.

5. They desire to inhabit the bodies of animals if they can't inhabit a person.

The country in which this man lived was inhabited by many Gentiles. (Jews were not supposed to keep swine.) When the unclean spirits went into the two thousand swine, the swine became crazed. They ran down into the sea and were drowned.

CONTRAST OF THE LEPER AND THE DEMON-POSSESSED MAN

Jesus sent the leper to the priest in Jerusalem and said he should tell *no one* along the way (Sp-28), but He told the other man to go to his house and tell his family about the great things the Lord had done for him and how He had had mercy on him. The man who had been demon-possessed obeyed Jesus and published throughout the whole area of Decapolis what the Lord had done for him. The people marveled; but the local people, seeing the man healed and their pigs drowned in the sea, asked the Lord to leave. He and His disciples returned to Capernaum.

FOUR MIRACLES IN CAPERNAUM

As soon as Jesus arrived on the other side, word came to Him that the daughter of Jairus, one of the rulers of the synagogue, was at the point of death. A great multitude thronged about Jesus on His way to Jairus' house. A woman who had been ill for twelve years pushed through the crowd and touched His garment. She thought that if she could only touch His garment, she would be healed. Jesus honored her faith, even though it was very imperfect, and healed her. There was nothing magical about His robe, but this seems to illustrate the high value that Jesus put upon faith. Even though the woman didn't understand how, she believed that Jesus would heal her.

There is a similarity between this incident and two that are found in the book of Acts. Some people moved their sick so that Peter's shadow would fall upon them (Acts 5:15). Others carried handkerchiefs (cloths that had come in contact with Paul's body) to sick people in order that they might be healed (Acts 19:11-12).

SECOND RESTORATION TO LIFE

Jairus' daughter had died before Jesus got to the house, but Jesus restored her to life.

TWO BLIND MEN AND A DUMB DEMONIAC

Upon leaving Jairus' house, two blind men called to Jesus, "Have mercy on us, thou son of David." By this expression they acknowledged their faith in Jesus as the Messiah. He in turn said unto them, "According to your faith be it done unto you."

As they left, Jesus freed a dumb demon-possessed man from the demon. The multitude marveled, but the Pharisees still said that Jesus was casting out demons by the prince of demons.

RECEPTION AND REJECTION OF CHRIST

Because of the rejection of some people, Jesus was now teaching in parables. The owners of the swine valued their property more than they did the healing of this demon-possessed man who inhabited the graveyard. While the multitudes marveled at Jesus' wonderful works, more and more people recognized that this was the Son of David, the promised Messiah. But the Pharisees refused to accept Him.

MEMORY HELPS

The activities of this period centered around the Sea of Galilee. The key word is SEA. Jesus gave the kingdom of heaven parables *by the sea*. Crossing to the other side, He stilled the tempest *on the sea*. When they got to the *other side of the sea*, He healed the demoniac in the graveyard; and the demons left the man, went into the swine, and drove the swine *into the sea*. When Jesus was asked to leave, He crossed *back over the sea* to Capernaum and performed the four miracles there. Capernaum is located on the northwest shore of the *Sea of Galilee*.

WHAT GOD IS LIKE

His power: He clearly demonstrated His power over the winds and the sea, over demons, disease and death.

His long-suffering: He protected His disciples when their faith was faltering during the storm, and He honored the faith of the woman who touched His garment.

His compassion: He responded to the sorrowing faith of Jairus by raising his daughter. What an encouragement the vibrant faith of the two blind men must have been to Him.

QUESTIONS FOR MEDITATION

1. After all the miracles the disciples had seen Christ perform, they were still amazed that nature would obey Him. Do you consciously or subconsciously limit the power of God?

2. The demon-possessed man in the graveyard returned home and told his friends and neighbors what wonderful things Christ had done for him. Have you done the same?

3. The woman who touched Christ's garment had an imperfect faith. How much of your understanding of spiritual things is based on superstition or human ideas? Are you systematically studying the Word so that your faith is based on the Bible?

4. Jesus opened the physical eyes of the blind. Have you asked Him to open your spiritual understanding so that you can learn about Him and His plan for your life?
5. The demon-possessed man couldn't speak, and Jesus made it possible for him to do so. Do you think that Jesus could help you learn to speak for Him? Are you willing to let Him?

See Appendix P.

CHAPTER 11

SECOND REJECTION AT NAZARETH

SPRING OF A.D. 29

KEY WORD: 212.

Key Events	Matthew	Mark	Luke
1. Second rejection at Nazareth	13:54-58	6:1-6	
2. Twelve sent forth two by two (fourth Galilean tour)	9:35— 11:1	6:6-13	9:1-6
3. John the Baptist's death (Machaerus)	14:1-12	6:14-29	9:7-9

Read at least the fullest account of each event.
Locate the key events on the map in Appendix G.

SECOND REJECTION AT NAZARETH

Jesus returned one last time to Nazareth and taught again in the synagogue, but the people would not accept Him. The Scriptures say that because of their unbelief He only performed a few miracles and He marveled at their unbelief (Mark 6:5-6).

78

KINGDOM PROCLAIMED ON THE FOURTH GALILEAN TOUR

Jesus sent the apostles out two by two into Galilee. They were to proclaim that the kingdom of heaven was at hand (Matt. 10:7). As King, He delegated to them authority over unclean spirits, all manner of sickness and disease, and death (Matt. 11:1-10).

As they went they were not to make special provision for their material necessities. God would supply this through the people to whom they ministered. Jesus told them, "He that receiveth you receiveth me; and he that receiveth me receiveth him that sent me" (Matt. 10:40). After the apostles had left, Jesus Himself went into their cities to preach. Jesus told His disciples not to go to the Gentiles or the Samaritans but rather to the lost sheep of the house of Israel. God had promised Israel a king. The kingdom was being offered to Israel.

DEATH OF JOHN THE BAPTIST

John the Baptist was beheaded by Herod the Tetrarch (Antipas). He had been imprisoned in Herod's castle at Machaerus in Peraea for almost two years. He had boldly told Herod that he should not be living with his brother's wife, Herodias. She wasn't content to have John in jail; and when the opportunity presented itself, she tricked Herod into beheading him.

RECEPTION AND REJECTION OF CHRIST

When Jesus returned to Nazareth and taught and performed miracles, the people asked the following questions: (1) Where did He learn these things? (2) Where did His wisdom come from? (3) How did He do these things (Matt. 13:54, 57)?

When they attempted to answer the question "Who is Jesus?" they justified their unbelief with the following answers: (1) This is the carpenter's son. (2) He was a carpenter among us. (3) Mary is His mother. (4) His brothers and sisters are here (Mark 6:3). Jesus told them that a prophet is honored except in his own country, in his own house, and by his own relatives.

MEMORY HELPS

The memory key in this period is 212.; the first 2 stands for the second rejection in Nazareth. The 12 represents the twelve apostles being sent out two by two over Galilee. Just as a period is used at the end of a sentence, so this period after the number 212 represents the end of John the Baptist's life.

THE LIFE OF JOHN THE BAPTIST

John's life can be visually represented on the time chart. Here is a list of the six major events in the life of John:

1. His birth about six months before Jesus' birth
2. His ministry beginning in S-26
3. Baptizing Jesus in F-26
4. Carrying on a parallel ministry with Jesus in Judaea and then being imprisoned in S-27
5. While in prison, sending his disciples to inquire if Jesus was the Messiah in S-28
6. His death in Sp-29

If these numbers are placed in the proper spot on the chart and are connected with a line, they form the letter *J*. *J* stands for John.

WHAT GOD IS LIKE

His mercy: Jesus returned to Nazareth a second time to try to reach the people. They had rejected Him and even attempted to kill Him (Sp-28).

His power: He delegated power and authority to His disciples. When He commands, He enables His servants to obey Him.

80

His provision: He told His disciples not to worry about food, clothing or lodging. This was His responsibility. He worked in the hearts of the people, and they provided for His disciples.

QUESTIONS FOR MEDITATION

1. Jesus returned a second time to Nazareth even though they had tried to kill Him. Have you classified certain people as unreachable? Are you willing to go to them one more time?
2. John the Baptist invested his life in the service of God. Have you ever seriously considered whether you would be willing to do this?
3. Jesus provided for His apostles' needs. Do you think He will still do this today?
4. Jesus gave His apostles the spiritual enablement to carry out His ministry. Are you trusting Him to do the same for you today?

CHAPTER 12

FEEDING THE MULTITUDES

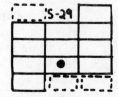

SUMMER OF A.D. 29

KEY WORD: FOOD

Key Events	Matthew	Mark	Luke	John
1. Feeding of the 5,000 (north of the Sea of Galilee)	14:13-23	6:30-46	9:10-17	6:1-15
Walking on the water	14:24-36	6:47-56		6:16-21
Bread of life discourse (Capernaum)				6:22-71
Eating with unwashed hands (Capernaum)	15:1-20	7:1-23		
2. Daughter of Syrophoenician healed (Phoenicia)	15:21-28	7:24-30		
Deaf and dumb man healed		7:31-37		
3. Feeding of the 4,000 (Decapolis)	15:29-38	8:1-9		
Pharisees and Sadducees seek a sign	15:39—16:4	8:10-12		
Jesus warns disciples against false teaching	16:5-12	8:13-21		
Blind man healed at Bethsaida		8:22-26		

Key Events	Matthew	Mark	Luke	John
4. Peter's good confession (on journey to Mount Hermon)	16:13-20	8:27-30	9:18-21	
Jesus foretells death, resurrection and second coming	16:21-28	8:31— 9:1	9:22-27	
5. Transfiguration (Mount Hermon)	17:1-13	9:2-13	9:28-36	
Demon-possessed boy (Mount Hermon)	17:14-20	9:14-29	9:37-43	
Foretells death and resurrection (on way to Galilee)	17:22-23	9:30-32	9:43-45	
6. Coin in fish's mouth (Capernaum)	17:24-27			
Instructions to followers: childlike simplicity, forgiveness, dedication	18:1-35	9:33-50	9:46-62	

Read at least the fullest account of each event.

Locate each of the key events on the map in Appendix G.

FEEDING OF THE FIVE THOUSAND

This miracle is the only one recorded in all four gospels. When the disciples had returned from their tour of Galilee and reported their experiences to Jesus, He asked them to come apart with Him to a desert place; but the multitudes followed them. Jesus had compassion on them because they were like sheep without a shepherd, so He taught them. At the close of the day, the disciples suggested that Jesus send the people away so that they could go into the villages and get something to eat. Instead, Jesus commanded His disciples to feed them.

PROVISION FOR SERVICE

There are some basic principles of service illustrated in this miracle:

83

1. *Obeying the command* (Matt. 14:16). You must be willing and ready to obey the Lord's commands. In this case, "Give ye them to eat."

2. *Recognizing limitations* (Mark 6:37). The ability or enablement for the task cannot be purchased with money. They didn't have enough money to buy food.

3. *Taking inventory* (Mark 6:38). You need to examine the gifts and abilities God has given you. They found five loaves and two fishes.

4. *Giving all to Jesus* (Matt. 14:18). You need to dedicate what you have to Him. The little boy gave his food to Jesus to use.

5. *Resting in faith* (John 6:10). Jesus had the disciples arrange the crowd in an orderly manner on the ground. This was done with every expectation of the people's being fed.

6. *Giving thanks and sharing* (Matt. 14:19). This is the Lord's part, taking what you have given Him and, with a heavenly blessing, preparing it or making it usable and giving it back to you.

7. *Receiving the bread* (Matt. 14:19). In faith appropriate the provision that the Lord has for the occasion.

8. *Feeding the multitude* (Matt. 14:19). Distribute to the multitude what the Lord has given you with full assurance that the need will be met and all will "be filled" (Mark 6:42).

Notice the difference between this miracle and the manna that was given to the children of Israel. God provided manna directly to the Israelites, but on this occasion He used human instruments to supply the need and distribute to the people.

A POPULAR POLITICAL MOVEMENT REJECTED

The people became enthusiastic after Jesus fed the five thousand; and "when Jesus therefore perceived that they would come and take him by force, to make him a king, he departed again into a mountain himself alone" (John 6:15). Jesus offered the children of Israel a kingdom—a kingdom

84

that God would set up on earth. He did not come to accept a kingdom from men. Jesus knew their hearts and knew that they wanted Him, not because He was the son of David, the promised Messiah, but because He had provided bread so their stomachs were filled.

WALKING ON WATER

Jesus sent His disciples back across the lake to Capernaum while He went up on a mountain to pray. This incident illustrates four principles concerning the climate of Christian service:

1. *The will of God* (Mark 6:45). The disciples were where the Lord wanted them. He had "constrained" them to enter the boat.

2. *Jesus' concern* (Mark 6:48).

3. *Conflict with evil* (Mark 6:48). The wind was contrary to them. Just because Jesus had sent them didn't mean that it must be smooth sailing.

4. *God's faithfulness.* He is willing to help—miraculously if necessary (Mark 6:48-52). Jesus came walking on the sea and would have passed by them, but they cried out to Him and asked Him into the boat. He will not force His help upon you.

In summary, as you serve the Lord, you need to be certain that you are in His will. You can be encouraged, for He is aware of any problem which you have. You should expect conflict and rejoice because Jesus is willing and eager to help.

When Peter saw the Lord walking on the water, he wanted to do likewise. This was a supernatural thing, and he did walk on the water as long as he kept his eyes on the Lord. But even when he became distracted by the wind and the violent storm, the Lord was there to help him.

The Christian life is a supernatural life. You are expected to live a holy life, a life that is different from the world. But by yourself you can't live this kind of life any more than you

85

can walk on water. The good news is that the Lord wants to help you, and He will help you live victoriously as long as you walk in faith depending on Him. If you fall into sin, He is ready to lift you back up (I John 1:9).

BREAD OF LIFE DISCOURSE

In the synagogue at Capernaum Jesus gave a very important discourse on the bread of life. Jesus had become very popular, but He told the people in John 6:26, "Ye seek me, not because ye saw the miracles, but because ye did eat of the loaves, and were filled." They wanted to know what they should do to work the works of God; and He answered, "This is the work of God, that ye believe on him whom he hath sent" (John 6:29). This discourse has some difficult portions, but the heart of the message seems to be in the following verses:

"Then Jesus said unto them, Verily, verily, I say unto you, Moses gave you not that bread from heaven; but my Father giveth you the true bread from heaven. For the bread of God is he which cometh down from heaven, and giveth life unto the world. Then said they unto him, Lord, evermore give us this bread. And Jesus said unto them, I am the bread of life: he that cometh to me shall never hunger; and he that believeth on me shall never thirst" (John 6:32-35).

"It is the spirit that quickeneth; the flesh profiteth nothing: the words that I speak unto you, they are spirit, and they are life" (John 6:63).

THE TRUE BREAD

Jesus made four promises for this true bread: (1) It satisfies—you will never hunger or thirst (John 6:35). (2) It will give you eternal life (John 6:50-51, 54, 58). (3) It promises resurrection (John 6:54). (4) It gives fellowship with Christ—a mutual indwelling (John 6:56).

In His discourse Jesus was correcting three popular errors of His followers:

1. Materialism (John 6:27). They were seeking "the meat which perishes."

2. Legalism (John 6:28-29). He taught them that the work of God is not *doing* but *believing*.

3. Unbelief. Even though they had seen the miracle of the feeding of the 5,000, they still asked for miracles.

THE DISPUTE OVER HAND-WASHING

One of the strongest traditions observed by the scribes and the Pharisees during the life of Christ was the ceremonial hand-washing. It was a part of the unwritten oral law handed down from one generation to the next. There were two great rabbinical schools in Judaea at the time. They were led by the teachers Hillel and Shammai. They normally argued and disputed about almost everything, but they were in agreement on one thing: hand-washing. (See Appendix E.) The Pharisees condemned Jesus for not ceremonially washing His hands, but Jesus called them hypocrites and showed them that their traditions actually caused them to break the commandments of God (Matt. 15:3, 6). Jesus explained in Matthew 15:18-20 that the things that proceed out of the heart of man defile him, rather than the lack of ceremonial washings.

THIRD LONG-DISTANCE HEALING

Jesus left Galilee and went up the coast into Phoenicia. When a woman that had a demon-possessed daughter came up to Him, she said, "Have mercy on me, O Lord, thou son of David; my daughter is grievously vexed with a devil" (Matt. 15:22). Son of David was a title given to the promised King of Israel. But Jesus answered and said, "I am not sent but unto the lost sheep of the house of Israel" (Matt. 15:24). As the promised King, or the Messiah, who in His kingdom would banish the powers of evil, He did not offer a kingdom to the Phoenicians but only to Israel. But, in His grace and compassion, He did heal the woman's daughter. Jesus told her that because of her faith, her daughter was healed; and when she returned home, she found that this was true. Jesus did not go to the daughter nor did the daughter see Jesus—a long-distance healing.

Jesus returned above the northern part of Galilee, swinging through the kingdom ruled by Herod Philip II into the area known as Decapolis and to the eastern shore of the Sea of Galilee. On the way He healed a deaf and dumb man.

FEEDING THE FOUR THOUSAND

Jesus performed a second miraculous feeding of a multitude. Mark and Matthew have recorded both of these miracles of feeding the multitudes.

Note the differences between them:

Differences	5,000	4,000
Number of days the multitude had been with Jesus	1 day	3 days
Food Jesus used	5 loaves and 2 fishes	7 loaves and a few small fishes
Amount of food left over	12 baskets	7 baskets
Place where feeding occurred	north of the Sea of Galilee	southeast of the Sea of Galilee
Number of men fed	5,000	4,000

Even the two words translated "baskets" in our King James Version are different in Greek. The seven baskets used at the feeding of the four thousand were a much larger type of basket. Sometimes they were even large enough to hold a man. The other word was usually used to speak of a basket that was carried in the hand.

WARNING AGAINST FALSE TEACHING

Jesus and His disciples went across the sea. While in the boat He warned His disciples against the leaven of the Pharisees and the Sadducees. The disciples didn't understand what He meant. He explained that He was warning them against the false teaching of the Pharisees and the Sadducees (see Appendix R). Landing on the north shore of the Sea of Galilee, Jesus and His disciples walked north through Bethsaida where He healed a blind man. This was an unusual miracle because it was not an instantaneous cure, but came in two stages.

REJECTION OF JESUS IN THE FOURTH GALILEAN TOUR

As they journeyed north toward Mount Hermon, Jesus asked His disciples, who had been on the preaching tour of Galilee, "Who do men say that I am?" Some said that He was John the Baptist, Elijah, Jeremiah or one of the prophets. They thought He was a great man but not the promised son of David, King of Israel, the Messiah. They did not receive Him (John 1:11).

THE GREAT CONFESSION

"He saith unto them, But whom say ye that I am? And Simon Peter answered and said, Thou art the Christ, the Son of the living God" (Matt. 16:15-16).

In Jesus' response there is a play on words. He says, "And I say also unto thee, That thou art Peter, and upon this rock I will build my church; and the gates of hell shall not prevail against it. And I will give unto thee the keys of the kingdom of heaven: and whatsoever thou shalt bind on earth shall be bound in heaven: and whatsoever thou shalt loose on earth shall be loosed in heaven" (Matt. 16:18-19). Peter (*petros*) means "a little rock"; and the word translated rock (*petra*) means "a massive rock." Jesus did not say that He would build the church upon Peter but on the confession that Peter made. No one can scripturally consider that he is a part of the church unless he believes that Jesus is the Christ, the Messiah, the Saviour promised in the Old Testament, the Son of the living God.

This conversation also teaches something else very important. The church was still in the future at this time, a mystery or unrevealed truth (Eph. 3:3-6; 5:25-32). Jesus said, "I will build my church."

THE KEYS

Jesus promised that He would give them the keys of the kingdom of heaven. He later told the scribes that they had taken away the keys of the kingdom from the people. The key that provides entrance into the kingdom (as well as into heaven) is a personal faith in Jesus as the Christ, the Son of the living God. By this faith, man is born again.

The scribes or rabbis of that day considered that they were the interpreters of the law and that they were the ones that told the people what they could and could not do. This is what the expression "binding and loosing" means—giving permission or forbidding certain things. Jesus did not give Peter the power to admit people to heaven or keep them from heaven. The literal translation would read like this: "Whatsoever thou shalt bind [forbid] on earth shall already have been bound [forbidden] in heaven: and whatsoever thou shalt loose [permit] on earth shall already have been loosed [permitted] in heaven." The words *bound* and *loosed* are in the perfect tense in Greek.

JESUS FORETOLD HIS DEATH AND RESURRECTION

When Jesus told His disciples that He was going to be killed, He wasn't just thinking that He *might* be killed. He told them the details of His death: (1) It would be in Jerusalem. (2) He would be rejected by the elders, the chief priests and the scribes. (3) He would be killed. (4) On the third day He would rise again.

Peter rebuked Jesus for talking about dying. It had only been a short time before this when the Lord had commended him for his good confession. Jesus said that the knowledge that He was the Christ had been revealed to Peter by His

90

Father in heaven. Now He rebuked Peter and said, "Get thee behind me, Satan: for thou savourest not the things that be of God, but the things that be of men" (Mark 8:33). This should be a warning to all Christians not to allow Satan to use them to spread his message. It was only a short time from the good confession to this rebuke.

TEACHING ABOUT THE SECOND COMING

The disciples didn't understand the significance of what Christ promised when He said that some of His disciples would not taste of death until they saw the Son of man coming in His kingdom. Six days later a preview of the coming of Christ in His glory to set up His kingdom was given to Peter, James and John on the mount of transfiguration.

THE TRANSFIGURATION

Jesus took Peter, James and John up on a high mountain, probably Mount Hermon. There He was transfigured before them. This had a lasting impression on them. Many years later, Peter spoke of this in his second epistle (II Peter 1:16-18). The Bible gives a little glimpse, on the mount of transfiguration, of what Jesus will look like at His second coming.

A person is born again when he receives Jesus Christ as his personal Saviour but often his life does not appear any different to those around him. There are similarities in the transfiguration episode and in the life of a Christian who grows in grace and learns to walk in close fellowship with God:

1. *Jesus prayed* (Luke 9:28). The Christian who learns to walk in fellowship with God will spend time in prayer.

2. *Jesus' face began to shine* (Matt. 17:2). People will become aware of the new radiance about the life of the Christian who walks in the fellowship with God.

3. *Jesus' garments changed* (Matt. 17:2). A Christian often changes the way he dresses so that he will not be a reproach to Christ.

4. *Jesus had new companions, Moses and Elijah* (Luke 9:30). A Christian will often make new friends. His old companions will misunderstand him and many times dislike being with him because he doesn't like to participate in the things that they do (I Peter 4:3-4).

5. *Jesus talked with Moses and Elijah about His death* (Luke 9:31). The talk of a Christian becomes different. The work of Christ on the cross becomes very important.

6. *The disciples were sleepy* (Luke 9:32). Even the Christian who is walking in close fellowship with God needs to guard against "drowsiness," disinterest in spiritual things.

7. *Peter had plans to build three tabernacles* (Luke 9:33). The Christian who is walking with God will be seeking to glorify God, not merely making plans of his own (see Matt. 9:35).

THE DISCIPLES FAILED TO CAST OUT A DEMON

While Jesus was on the mount of transfiguration, a father brought his son to the disciples; and they could not cast out the demon. Jesus later explained to His disciples that this kind came out only by prayer. (The better Greek manuscripts omit the words "and fasting" from Mark 9:29.) The Christian is involved in a spiritual warfare. Ephesians 6:12 says, "For we wrestle not against flesh and blood, but against principalities, against powers, against the rulers of the darkness of this world, against spiritual wickedness in high places." Daniel 10:12-14 gives a hint of this spiritual warfare. On the way back to Capernaum Jesus again foretold His death and resurrection. The disciples still didn't understand, but they were afraid to ask Him to explain it.

THE ATTITUDE OF A DISCIPLE

The remaining incidents in this period seem to center around the attitude Jesus expected of His disciples.

1. The miracle of the coin in the fish's mouth teaches that even though Jesus didn't have to pay the temple tax because of who He was—the very God of the temple—He

provided a coin for Peter to pay the tax for both of them in order that this might not be a stumbling block to others. This teaching about stumbling blocks is expanded in I Corinthians 8 and in Romans 14.

2. In Luke 9:46, the disciples were arguing about who should be the greatest in the kingdom. In order to teach them humility, Jesus called a little child to Him and said, "Whosoever therefore shall humble himself as this little child, the same is greatest in the kingdom of heaven" (Matt. 18:4).

3. The disciples saw a man casting out demons in Jesus' name but they told him to stop because he was not following with them. Jesus said, "He that is not against us is on our part" (Mark 9:38-40).

4. In Matthew 18:15-35, Jesus told how one brother should forgive another and what the proper relationship should be between them.

5. In Luke 9:57-62 Jesus taught that if you know that God has called you to follow Him, nothing should hinder you—neither hardship, nor family nor friends.

CHILDREN AND JESUS

Jesus revealed a special love for children (Mark 9:36). It appears that God has assigned a special angel to each one (Matt. 18:10). A special responsibility is assigned to parents or anyone who works with children: "But whoso shall offend one of these little ones which believe in me, it were better for him that a millstone were hanged about his neck, and that he were drowned in the depth of the sea" (Matt. 18:6). "Even so it is not the will of your Father which is in heaven, that one of these little ones should perish" (Matt. 18:14).

RECEPTION AND REJECTION OF JESUS

Jesus attracted a multitude after He fed the five thousand; but after He gave His bread of life discourse, many of His disciples or followers left and walked no more with Him (John 6:66). Because Jesus wouldn't keep the traditions

93

of the Pharisees, they became all the more angry. The Syrophoenician woman was commended for her faith. Jesus said, "Great is thy faith." The four thousand glorified the God of Israel because of the teaching and healings that Jesus performed (Matt. 15:31). This was in the very area that Jesus sent the demon-possessed man from the graveyard after he was healed. The response of these people may have been due to the work of this man.

MEMORY HELPS

The key word for this period is FOOD. The first incident is the *feeding* of the five thousand. Then, after sending the disciples back to Capernaum, Jesus walked on the water. The next event was the *bread* of life discourse. This was followed by the dispute of the Pharisees over ceremonial handwashing before *eating*. The next key event was the healing of the Syrophoenician's daughter. The woman admitted that it wasn't right to give children's (Israelites') *bread* to the dogs (Gentiles), but she said that the dogs do eat the *crumbs* that fall under the table. The next event was the *feeding* of the four thousand; and in the boat trip that followed, Jesus warned against the *leaven* of the Pharisees and the Sadducees. The events that followed do not have anything to do with food, but they all center around a trip up to the mount of transfiguration and back. In Capernaum, there was the miracle of the coin in the *fish's mouth*.

If the two fishes are laid on top of the adjacent map of Palestine, their outlines will look approximately like the travels of Jesus and His disciples during this period. If the five little loaves are put on the map in the proper place, they will indicate the five locations where food is specifically mentioned in this period. (You must remember that the fishes the little boy carried were probably quite small and not like the ones used on the map. The lunch probably would be similar to sardines and biscuits.)

94

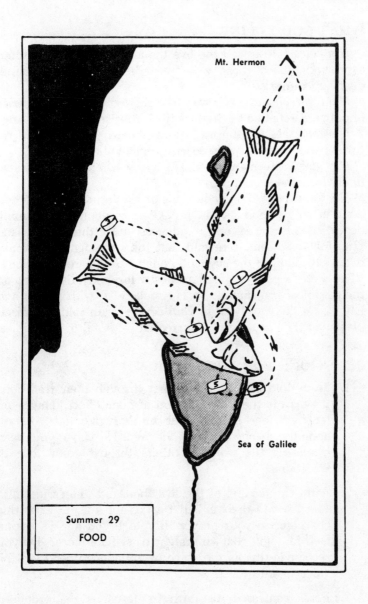

Mt. Hermon

Sea of Galilee

Summer 29
FOOD

95

WHAT GOD IS LIKE

His power: Jesus fed the five thousand and the four thousand and healed those who were demon-possessed, blind, deaf and dumb.

His righteousness: His was true righteousness, not a series of outward acts like the hypocritical Pharisees' righteousness.

His love: He fed the multitudes, healed the sick, and returned the demon-possessed children to their parents.

His glory: He manifested His glory when He was transfigured on the mountain.

His knowledge: His knowledge of the future was very evident in this period as He talked more about His coming death. The Pharisees and Sadducees in Matthew 16:1 asked Him for a sign but were told that the only sign they would receive would be the sign of Jonah (Jesus' resurrection). After Peter's good confession, Jesus foretold His death; on the mount of transfiguration He spoke of it with Moses and Elijah; on the way back to Galilee He again told His disciples about His death and resurrection—a total of four times.

QUESTIONS FOR MEDITATION

1. Jesus told the Pharisees that through their traditions they made the Word of God of none effect. Have you let traditions hinder your ministry so that you are actually disobedient to the Word? Have you been hindering the work of others through your love of traditions?

2. After the feeding of the five thousand, the scribes and Pharisees in their unbelief asked for a sign. Does this characterize your prayer life? Are you always asking God for signs that you might trust Him more? Do you recognize this as the voice of unbelief rather than the voice of faith?

3. Peter confessed his faith in Jesus as the promised Saviour. Have you told Jesus that you believe in Him

as Saviour? Have you confessed Him before men or are you "a secret disciple"?

4. Peter, James and John saw Jesus transfigured before them. Have your friends and family noticed that you have had a life-changing experience? Does your life reflect a little of the glory of Christ?

5. Jesus had Peter pay the temple tax in order that He might not be a stumbling block to others. Are you careful in not causing others to stumble?

See Appendix E.

CHAPTER 13

LIVING WATER

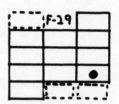

FALL OF A.D. 29

KEY WORD: SERVING

Key Events	Luke	John
1. **T** abernacles Feast (Jerusalem)		7:1—8:1
Adulterous woman		8:2-11
Jesus the light of the world		8:12-59
Man born blind healed		9:1-41
Good Shepherd discourse		10:1-21
2. **S** eventy sent out (Judaea)	10:1-24	
Good Samaritan parable	10:25-37	
Supper at Mary and Martha's (Bethany)	10:38-42	
Disciples taught to pray	11:1-13	
3. **A** ccused of league with Beelzebub, Jesus		
healed dumb demoniac	11:14-36	
4. **E** ating with a Pharisee, Jesus:		
Denounced hypocrisy (Judaea)	11:37-54	
Told parables on service	12:1—13:9	
Healed a crippled woman	13:10-21	
5. **F** east of Dedication (Jerusalem)		10:22-39

Read Luke 10–13 and John 7–10. It is easy to remember where these events are located in the Bible: chapters 7–10 in John, and 10–13 in Luke.

THE FEAST OF TABERNACLES

This period began with the Feast of Tabernacles and ended with the Feast of Dedication. "Because the Jews sought to kill him" (John 7:1), Jesus went up secretly to Jerusalem. The Feast of Tabernacles commemorated the wanderings of

98

the children of Israel in the wilderness. By the time of Christ's ministry, quite a ritual had developed. On the last day of the feast, the priest went down to the pool of Siloam and brought a golden pitcher of water into the temple. This was brought to the altar and poured out as the regular morning sacrifice was being offered.

In an atmosphere of trumpet blasts, marching priests, the chanting of psalms, fine priestly garments and animal sacrifices within the beautiful temple, Jesus stood and cried, saying, "If any man thirst, let him come unto me, and drink. He that believeth on me, as the scripture hath said, out of his belly shall flow rivers of living water" (John 7:37-38).

Some people had turned to ritualism for spiritual satisfaction. The elements of worship that should have pointed to Jesus the Saviour were being used for their own beauty, and He was being ignored and rejected. But for those people who realized they had an emptiness in their life, He gave a three-fold solution:

1. *Thirst.* There must be a desire for something more, for a reality to life, for a Christlike life, for the Holy Spirit's guidance and power (John 7:39).

2. *Come and drink.* This is the act by which the believer claims Christ's promise for His own.

3. *Believe on Christ.* This is the final part, trusting (believing) that Christ will do what He has promised. The person who thirsts, comes to Christ and drinks, and trusts Him will have a more meaningful life as he is filled by the Spirit of God. This was a life-transforming promise that Jesus made but many still rejected Him. Some could not believe that Jesus was the Christ because they said that He had come out of Galilee. They knew from the Scriptures that He was to come of the seed of David and from Bethlehem. They knew their Scriptures, but they did not take the trouble to examine the evidence about Jesus. Jesus warned them, "I said therefore unto you, that ye shall die in your sins: for if ye believe not that I am he, ye shall die in your sins" (John 8:24).

JESUS AND THE ADULTEROUS WOMAN

The scribes and Pharisees tried to trap Jesus. They brought a woman taken in adultery to Him to ask Him what should be done. The Romans at that time allowed the Jews a certain amount of self-government, but they did not allow them to put people to death. According to the Old Testament, both the man and the woman who committed adultery should be stoned to death. These men thought they had Jesus in a dilemma. No matter what He said, He would be in trouble. If He said they should go ahead and stone the woman, He would be in trouble with the Roman government. If He said not to stone her, He would be in trouble with the people because the Jews would then say that He was against the law.

For any crime that the law deemed worthy of stoning, the witnesses were to cast the first stones. Jesus said unto the men, "He that is without sin among you, let him first cast a stone at her" (John 8:7). The Scriptures say that they were convicted by their own consciences, and one by one they left, starting with the eldest.

THE LIGHT OF THE WORLD

When Adam sinned, the world was plunged into darkness. In the following generations, man lost his knowledge of the true character of God and His standard of conduct for life. Jesus promised that those who followed Him would no longer walk in darkness. The chart tells what Christ said (1) about Himself, (2) about those who believe on Him and walk in the light, and (3) about those who reject Him and walk in darkness.

SIGHT FOLLOWS LIGHT

In John 8, Jesus gave the light of the world discourse. In John 9 He healed a man who was born blind. This healing was on the Sabbath, and it made the Pharisees very angry. They were more concerned with keeping the Sabbath according to their traditions than they were with this blind man receiving his sight.

THE GOOD SHEPHERD

Jesus declared that He was the good Shepherd in contrast to the false religious shepherds of Israel: "He that entereth not by the door into the sheepfold, but climbeth up some other way, the same is a thief and a robber. But he that entereth in by the door is the shepherd of the sheep. To him the porter, openeth; and the sheep hear his voice: and he calleth his own sheep by name, and leadeth them out" (John 10:1-3). Many false Christs had come before Jesus, but He entered by the door. He fulfilled Old Testament prophecy. Jesus said, "All that ever came before me are thieves and robbers. . . . The thief cometh not, but for to steal, and to kill, and to destroy: I am come that they might have life, and that they might have it more abundantly" (John 10:8-10). The good Shepherd leads the sheep, provides pasture and safety, and even gives His life for the sheep.

THE SHEPHERD GIVES HIS LIFE FOR THE SHEEP

Jesus was aware that the cross lay before Him, but He clearly stated that no one was going to take His life from Him. He was going to lay it down so that He might take it up again (John 10:18).

SEVENTY SENT OUT

 In Sp-29 Jesus had sent out the twelve two by two to proclaim the kingdom of God. The twelve were sent out over Galilee. It is hard to tell exactly where the seventy went, but probably most of them went to Judaea because they went into every city and place where Jesus was about to visit.

101

"I AM THE LIGHT OF THE WORLD"

JOHN 8:12

UNBELIEVERS

1. Walk in darkness, v. 12
2. Don't know Christ, vv. 14, 19
3. Don't know the Father, vv. 19, 55
4. Die in their sins, vv. 21, 24
5. Of this world, v. 23
6. Crucify Christ, vv. 28, 37
7. Servant of sin, v. 34
8. Claim to be of God, v. 41
9. Can't understand spiritual things, v. 43
10. Devil is their father, v. 44
11. Do what the devil desires, v. 44
12. Don't believe Christ, vv. 45, 46
13. Not of God, v. 47
14. Dishonor Christ, v. 49
15. Liars, v. 55

BELIEVERS

1. Follow Christ, v. 12
2. Have light of life, v. 12
3. Not die in sins, v. 24
4. Believe on Jesus, v. 30
5. Continue in His Word, v. 31
6. Know the truth, v. 32
7. Free in Christ, v. 32
8. Love Christ, v. 42
9. Hear the words of God, v. 47
10. Not see death, v. 51

102

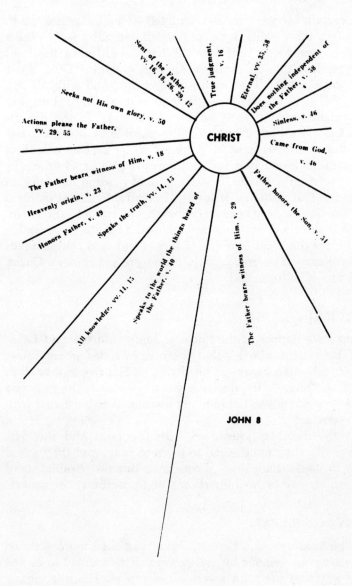

Sent of the Father,
vv. 16, 18, 26, 29, 12

True judgment,
v. 16

Eternal, vv. 35, 58

Does nothing independent of
the Father, v. 58

Seeks not His own glory, v. 50

Sinless, v. 46

Actions please the Father,
vv. 29, 55

CHRIST

Came from God,
v. 46

The Father bears witness of Him, v. 18

Father honors the Son, v. 51

Heavenly origin, v. 23

Honors Father, v. 49

Speaks the truth, vv. 14, 15

Speaks to the world the things heard of
the Father, v. 40

The Father bears witness of Him, v. 29

All knowledge, vv. 14, 15

JOHN 8

103

THE GOOD SAMARITAN

A certain lawyer (scribe) tempted Jesus by asking Him, "Master, what shall I do to inherit eternal life?" (Luke 10:25). Jesus said unto him, "What is written in the law? how readest thou?" And he answering said, "Thou shalt love the Lord thy God with all thy heart, and with all thy soul, and with all thy strength, and with all thy mind; and thy neighbour as thyself" (Luke 10:26-27). In the discussion that followed, Jesus told the parable of the good Samaritan to illustrate what it meant to be a good neighbor. By using a Samaritan rather than a scribe or Pharisee or priest or even a Levite, Jesus was able more graphically to show the real ministry of love. This parable also illustrates the ministry of Jesus who left heaven and came to the earth. He was despised and rejected of men (Isa. 53:3), but He Himself is the great example of love. "But God commendeth his love toward us, in that, while we were yet sinners, Christ died for us" (Rom. 5:8).

SERVING JESUS

Jesus ate supper at the home of Mary, Martha and Lazarus. He taught Martha that there were times when it was better to be like Mary, to be sitting at His feet rather than to be so "busy." If you have your eyes upon the one you serve, you are not so liable to get distracted or burdened with your serving.

As the disciples journeyed with the Lord and saw His prayer life, they too desired to learn to pray; and they asked Him to teach them how. Jesus gave them a parable about prayer, stressing the importance of importunity in prayer.

SERVING SATAN

After casting out a demon, Jesus was once more accused of casting out demons by evil powers. This seemed to be the only way that the unbelievers could explain His miracles.

HYPOCRITICAL SERVANTS

A Pharisee asked Jesus to eat with him. The Pharisees were very critical when Jesus did not ceremonially wash His hands. Jesus said that they were foolish and full of extortion and wickedness, and He strongly warned them about their hypocrisy. He told them that they put burdens on men that were too grievous to be borne. In their extreme legalism and many traditions, they had hidden the very meaning of the Scriptures. Jesus said, "Woe unto you, lawyers [scribes]! for ye have taken away the key of knowledge: ye entered not in yourselves, and them that were entering in ye hindered" (Luke 11:52). But instead of turning from their wickedness, the scribes and Pharisees only tried to trick Jesus into saying something that they might use to accuse Him (Luke 11:54).

SERVING SELF

Jesus told a parable about the rich fool who had a good harvest. His barns were not big enough so he tore them down and built bigger barns. He then said to himself, "I have much goods laid up for many years. Now I'll take it easy; I'll eat, drink and be merry." But then God said unto him, "Thou fool, this night thy soul shall be required of thee: then whose shall those things be, which thou hast provided?" (Luke 12:20).

Jesus then told a parable about a wise steward or servant who was faithfully performing his duties while his master was gone. He contrasted the wise servant with a foolish one who thought that his lord had delayed his coming. Consequently, he did not perform his duties; and the lord came back unexpectedly and found him in all his unfaithfulness!

SATAN'S SLAVE FREED

While teaching in the synagogue on the Sabbath day, Jesus healed a woman who had been sick for 18 years with some kind of affliction that kept her bowed over so that she could not stand up straight. The ruler of the synagogue was very angry because Jesus had healed on the Sabbath, but Jesus pointed out that each one of them would take their livestock out and water them. Wasn't it more important that this woman be healed whom "Satan had bound" for eighteen years?

THE FEAST OF DEDICATION

Jesus returned to Jerusalem for the Feast of Dedication which was in the winter. He was in the temple in Solomon's porch, and the Jews came around Him and asked Him to tell them plainly if He was the Christ. Jesus said, "I told you, and you wouldn't believe me nor the witness of my works." This made them very angry; and they took up stones to stone Him. They said, "Thou, being a man, makest thyself God" (John 10:33).

RECEPTION AND REJECTION OF CHRIST

If you could have taken a public opinion poll of the people of Judaea during the fall of A.D. 29 and asked the people this question, "What do you think of Jesus?" their response would have revealed these facts:

1. The religious Jews wanted to kill Him (John 7:1).
2. Jesus' brethren did not believe in Him (John 7:3-5).
3. Some people said, "He is a good man" (John 7:12).
4. Other people said, "He deceiveth the people" (John 7:12).
5. Some of the Jews couldn't understand how He could know all these things because He had had no formal rabbinical education (John 7:15).
6. Others said that Jesus had a demon (John 7:20).
7. Some people did not know. They wondered if the rulers knew that He was the Christ but had not told them (John 7:26-27).
8. Many believed that Jesus was the Christ (John 7:31).

9. Some of the multitude said that Jesus was the prophet that Moses prophesied would come (John 7:40).

10. Others were very certain that this was the Christ (John 7:41).

11. Others said that Christ would not come out of Galilee (John 7:41).

12. The officers who were sent to take Jesus, returned and said, "Never man spake like this man" (John 7:46).

13. The Pharisees and rulers very emphatically said that Jesus was not the Christ (John 7:47-48).

14. Nicodemus said that they ought to hear Him and see what He did before they judged Him (John 7:50-51).

SABBATH TRADITIONS

The miracle that Christ performed when He healed the blind man had no effect on the Pharisees. They said, "This man is not of God, because he keepeth not the sabbath day" (John 9:16). He didn't keep it according to their traditions so they would not receive Him.

The Scriptures record the progressive understanding of the blind man. When first asked about Jesus, he described Him as "a man that is called Jesus" (John 9:11). The second time he called Him a prophet (John 9:17). When Jesus later met the man, he acknowledged Him to be the Son of God (John 9:35-38).

The religious rulers put a lot of pressure on the people. They had already decided that if anyone confessed Jesus to be the Christ, he would be put out of the synagogue. After Jesus gave His Good Shepherd discourse, there was a division among the Jews. Some said that He was mad and had a demon. Others said that this could not be because a demon didn't talk like He did and couldn't open the eyes of the blind. In Luke 11:15 Jesus was again accused of casting out demons by evil powers. But His final rejection in this period came in John 10:33. The Jews wanted to kill Jesus because He said that He was God.

As Jesus approached the shadow of the cross, the division became greater. The questions "Who is Jesus?" and "What will I do with Him?" are questions that each person must answer for himself. A parent can't answer for a child or a child for a parent (Luke 12:51-53).

MEMORY HELPS

 The key word for this period is SERVING. This period began and ended with a feast. Perhaps it will help you remember the lesson if you think of a sandwich —the bread on top representing the first feast and the bottom slice, the last feast.

The first letter of the first word of each of the numbered key events from this period spell "feast" backward or from bottom to top. At a feast you usually think of not only the guests but also the *servants*. At the Feast of Tabernacles, Jesus found many people *serving* ritualism. The woman taken in adultery was a *servant* of sin. After His light of the world discourse, Jesus contrasted *servants* who walk in the light and *servants* who walk in the darkness. The blind man was a useless *servant*. Jesus contrasted the Good Shepherd with the *hireling* shepherd.

The next series of events occurred outside of Jerusalem, probably in Judaea. Seventy *servants* were sent out by Jesus. The good Samaritan *served* his neighbor while the priest and the Levite did not. At the supper at Mary, Martha and Lazarus' home, Martha was "cumbered" with her *serving*. Jesus was accused of being a *servant* of Beelzebub. The scribes and Pharisees were called hypocritical wicked *servants* by Jesus because they had taken away the key, and their traditions were hindering others. Jesus gave His series of parables about the rich fool who was *serving* self, the wise and foolish *servants,* and the barren fig tree which was of no *service* to its owner. The crippled woman He healed could be called Satan's *slave* because Jesus said that Satan had bound her.

WHAT GOD IS LIKE

His power: God's power was displayed many times as He healed and performed miracles. The enemy was not able to take Him because His time had not yet come.

His wrath: He warned the scribes and Pharisees and pointed out their hypocrisy in the strongest language.

His holiness: His holiness was stated in John 8:46.

His eternal character: He is eternal in character (John 8:35, 38).

His forgiveness: He told the woman taken in adultery to "go, and sin no more" (John 8:11). This is the third recorded incident where Jesus dealt with immoral women:

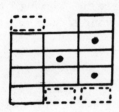

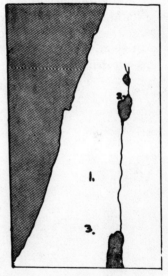

1. The woman at the well—F-27.
2. The woman who anointed Jesus' feet in Capernaum—S-28.
3. The woman taken in adultery in Jerusalem—F-29.

This is a real demonstration of the grace of God. There are three women of questionable morals in the genealogy of Christ: Tamar (Matt. 1:3), Rahab (Matt. 1:5), and Bathsheba, "her that had been the wife of Urias" (Matt. 1:6).

QUESTIONS FOR MEDITATION

1. Many Jewish people depended on ritualism for spiritual satisfaction. Do you depend on soft music, stained glass windows, carpets and choirs to take the place of real worship?
2. Does your heart "thirst" for reality? Are you willing to "come and drink" and "believe" that Christ will, through His Holy Spirit, make life real and meaningful for you?
3. The blind man couldn't explain everything about Jesus or how He had made him see, but he did testify to what he did know: "One thing I know, that, whereas I was blind, now I see" (John 9:25). Are you willing to testify about the things that you do know and not use the things that you don't know as an excuse to keep silent?
4. Martha allowed her serving of Jesus to become a distraction. Have you allowed your "serving" to take your eyes off Jesus so that your service has become a drudgery to you?

CHAPTER 14

RAISING THE DEAD

SPRING OF A.D. 30

KEY WORD: TRAVEL

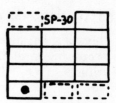

Key Events	Matthew	Mark	Luke	John
1. T eaching in Peraea, warned about Herod			13:22-35	10:40-42
Healed man of dropsy on Sabbath			14:1-6	
Parables on humility, rewards, excuses and discipleship			14:7-35	
Parables of the lost: sheep, coin, son and job			15:1— 16:18	
Rich man and Lazarus			16:19— 17:10	
2. R aised Lazarus from the dead (Bethany)				11:1-44
Jews counseled to kill Him (to Ephraim)				11:45-54
Ten lepers healed (Samaria, Galilee)			17:11-37	
3. A nswered prayer, divorce, little children	19:1-15	10:1-16	18:1-17	
Rich young ruler	19:16— 20:16	10:17-31	18:18-30	
Foretold death and resurrection	20:17-28	10:32-45	18:31-34	
4. V ery loud cry of blind men (Jericho)	20:29-34	10:46-52	18:35-43	
5. E ating at Zacchaeus' house (Jericho)			19:1-28	
6. L ast stop, second anointing (Bethany)	26:6-13	14:3-9		11:55— 12:8

111

Read at least the fullest account of each event.
See the map in Appendix G.

TEACHING IN PERAEA

Jesus spent most of this period teaching in Peraea. Luke records more of this period than any other of the gospel writers.

CHRIST AND THE PHARISEES

Most of the Pharisees were opposed to Jesus, but Luke 13:31 tells of certain Pharisees who came to warn Jesus that Herod (the Tetrarch) wanted to kill Him. A ruler of the Pharisees invited Jesus into his house to eat bread. It was on the Sabbath, and He healed a man with dropsy.

Jesus taught using a large number of parables. Among them were the great supper, building a tower, the lost sheep, the lost coin, the lost son, and the lost job.

THE WICKED NOT IN THE KINGDOM

Jesus again warned against mere profession of allegiance. When the hypocrites see Abraham, Isaac, Jacob and all the prophets in the kingdom of God but they themselves are cast forth, there will be much weeping and gnashing of teeth (Luke 13:28-30). Jesus also said that John the Baptist had been the first to preach the good news that the kingdom of God was at hand (Luke 16:16).

THE RICH MAN AND LAZARUS THE BEGGAR

Jesus pulled back the veil that hides life beyond the grave and told of two men that had died. This incident teaches several things:

1. There is life beyond the grave.
2. There is a place of blessing and a place of torment.
3. This will be a conscious experience.

4. Destinies are fixed in this life and will not be changed in the next.

5. The memory will continue to operate.

6. The people in Hades do not want to have their friends come there.

7. If people do not believe the Word of God, they would not pay attention to someone miraculously returned from the dead. This was proved a short time later when Christ restored life to Lazarus, the brother of Mary and Martha. Do not confuse Lazarus, the brother of Mary and Martha, with Lazarus the beggar.

LAZARUS RAISED FROM THE DEAD

Jesus had spent many hours in the house of His friends Mary, Martha and Lazarus. He had been ministering in Peraea; and, even after word came that Lazarus was sick, He waited until Lazarus had been dead four days before He arrived in Bethany. This miracle illustrates a very important lesson. Christians sometimes think of their loved ones and neighbors as hopeless sinners. They feel that they are too hard or wicked and that they will never become Christians. Lazarus' sisters thought that Jesus had waited too long. If He had only come, He could have healed their brother; but Lazarus was dead. They looked on the situation as hopeless. This incident illustrates several important truths about witnessing:

1. Jesus asked, "Where have you laid him?" They took Him to the tomb. You should take Christ to the "hopeless" sinner.

2. "Take away the stone," said Jesus. You should remove all hindrances and should not make it difficult for the sinner to receive Christ. Don't require that he do unscriptural things. For example, don't insist, "Come to church and be saved." (You don't have to be in a church building to be saved.)

113

3. "Lazarus, come forth!" Jesus called. There was power in the words of Jesus. You need to deliver the Word of God with faith and make it a personal invitation. Sinners are saved through believing the incorruptible Word of God (I Peter 1:23; Rom. 10:17).

4. "Loose him and let him go," commanded Jesus. Jesus had them unwind the graveclothes that were binding Lazarus. It is important to follow up new Christians, helping them break old habits and meet the attacks of the enemy.

It wasn't very long until the Jews wanted to kill not only Jesus but also Lazarus. A man had come from the grave, but the Pharisees did not listen to him. Because the Jews took counsel to kill Him, Jesus departed for Ephraim. This is thought to be located in the northern part of Judaea near the Samaritan border.

MURDER PLOTTED

The chief priests and the Pharisees gathered a council to decide what to do with Jesus. They acknowledged that He performed many miracles. "If we let him thus alone, all men will believe on him: and the Romans shall come and take away both our place and nation. And one of them, named Caiaphas, being the high priest that same year, said unto them, Ye know nothing at all, nor consider that it is expedient for us, that one man should die for the people, and that the whole nation perish not. And this spake he not of himself: but being high priest that year, he prophesied that Jesus should die for that nation; and not for that nation only, but that also he should gather together in one the children of God that were scattered abroad" (John 11:48-52). These religious rulers were plotting to keep the nation which they had, although in bondage to Rome, and to reject the kingdom that God had promised to them.

TEN LEPERS HEALED

 Two years earlier Jesus had healed a leper in Galilee and sent him as a testimony to the high priest. Now He healed ten more and told them to go show themselves to the priest. This was to be a ninefold testimony (for one was a Samaritan and would not go to the priest in Jerusalem). One healing might be explained away, but not nine. The Scriptures say that Jesus was going through Samaria and Galilee (Luke 17:11). This seems to be backward because Galilee is north of Samaria. Jesus knew that He was going to the cross, and He knew when He would be crucified. It appears that He left Ephraim and made His way north through Samaria, the southern part of Galilee, over to the Jordan Valley, and then down the traditional route that the Galileans traveled to Jerusalem. The next events in this period take place in Peraea.

WHEN WILL THE KINGDOM COME?

"And when he was demanded of the Pharisees, when the kingdom of God should come, he answered them and said, The kingdom of God cometh not with observation [outward show]: neither shall they say, Lo here! or, lo there! for, behold, the kingdom of God is within you [in the midst of you]" (Luke 17:20-21). The kingdom of God was present in the person of the King and a nucleus of citizens as represented by His disciples. Jesus promised the disciples that they would sit upon twelve thrones judging the twelve tribes of Israel in the kingdom (Matt. 19:28).

ANSWERED PRAYER, DIVORCE, AND LITTLE CHILDREN

As Jesus journeyed through Peraea, He taught about the importance of prayer, the proper attitude concerning divorce, and the faith of little children. This series is easy to

115

remember if you connect them all together in your thinking. In this age of rising divorce rates, if there was more prayer, there would be less divorce and fewer little children suffering because of broken homes.

People were bringing little children to Jesus, and the disciples stopped them. Mark 10:14 says, "But when Jesus saw it, he was much displeased, and said unto them, Suffer the little children to come unto me, and forbid them not: for of such is the kingdom of God." Some translations render the words "much displeased" as "moved with indignation."

A rich young ruler talked to Jesus. After he left, Jesus told His disciples how hard it is for rich people to be saved because it is so easy for them to "trust in riches."

JESUS FORETOLD HIS DEATH AND RESURRECTION

When Jesus said that they were going back to Jerusalem, the disciples were frightened. He explained that one of the reasons they were going was that the prophecies of the Old Testament might be fulfilled (Luke 18:31). He had told them before that He was going to die. This time He gave them additional details: (1) the chief priests and scribes would condemn Him to death, (2) He would be delivered to the Gentiles, (3) they would mock Him, (4) they would spit upon Him, (5) they would scourge Him and then kill Him, but (6) He would rise again in three days.

STATUS SEEKERS

Immediately following Jesus' prophecy of His coming death, the mother of James and John came to Jesus and asked Him that her sons might be chosen to sit one on His right hand and one on His left in His kingdom. This made the other disciples very angry. For about a year there had been at least some argument among them as to who would be the greatest. This is a good example of the self-centeredness of the human heart.

As Jesus journeyed toward Jerusalem, He passed through Jericho. There were two blind men sitting by the wayside. One of them seemed to do most of the talking. He heard that Jesus was going to pass nearby. He was helpless and couldn't come to Jesus. All he could do was cry out very loudly to Him. He used the expression "Son of David" which was a Messianic title for the promised Saviour. Many of the people around him rebuked him and tried to make him be quiet, but he only cried louder. Jesus heard the blind man and called to him and told him, "Go thy way, thy faith hath made thee whole."[1]

ZACCHAEUS IN A TREE

The little man Zacchaeus, a tax collector, climbed a tree so that he could see Jesus. A Pharisee would have nothing to do with a tax collector, but Jesus told Zacchaeus to come down from the tree. He said He was going to dine at his house that day. The Bible doesn't tell what went on in the house, but it does record the changed life of Zacchaeus.

THE SECOND COMING OF CHRIST

As Jesus neared the cross, He began to prepare His disciples for His rejection (see Luke 13:34-35; 17:24-25, 30) and His second coming. Jesus told a parable "because they thought that the kingdom of God should immediately appear" (Luke 19:11). He told about a certain nobleman who went into a *far country* to receive a kingdom for himself and *to return*. He called his ten servants, distributed ten pounds to them, and instructed them to trade with the pounds till he *returned*. When he *returned,* he called them to account and rewarded with authority in his kingdom according to their faithfulness. His enemies he destroyed.

This parable teaches many things, but Jesus' primary reason for telling it was so the disciples would understand that the kingdom was not going to be set up at that time.

117

LAST STOP, BETHANY

Six days before Passover, Jesus arrived in Bethany. Many people came out to see Him and Lazarus whom He had raised from the dead.

SECOND ANOINTING OF JESUS

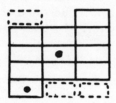

On Saturday evening at a supper, the second anointing of Jesus occurred. Of all His followers, Mary seemed to be the only one that understood that Jesus was about to die. When Judas complained about the high cost of the ointment (equal to a year's salary), Jesus said, "Let her alone: against the day of my burying hath she kept this" (John 12:7).

Compare the two anointings:

	First Anointing	*Second Anointing*
Time	Summer 28	Spring 30
Place	Capernaum	Bethany
Woman	A sinner	Mary
Home	A Pharisee	Simon the Leper
Reason	Thankfulness for forgiveness	Jesus' coming burial

RECEPTION AND REJECTION OF CHRIST

Like the wind of a storm, the crescendo of hatred seemed to be mounting against Christ. Many of the common people were turning to Him, but the religious rulers seemed to harden in their unbelief. They constantly plotted how they would kill Him. The rich young ruler chose his money instead of Christ. The Samaritan leper, the blind man and Zacchaeus did receive Christ.

MEMORY HELPS

The key word for this period is TRAVEL. Jesus' travels are shaped almost like a football. One point of the football is on Jerusalem and the other is in the Jordan Valley below the Sea of Galilee. His travels started in Peraea a little above the Dead Sea, went down to Bethany near Jerusalem, north to Ephraim, into Samaria and lower Galilee, and back down the Jordan Valley to Peraea, across the Jordan to Jericho, and ended in Bethany. The ten lepers were healed near the position of the football trademark on the map.

The first letter of the first word in each of the six series of key events spells out the word *travel*. It is very interesting to go through this series and notice the travels or "travel orders" that Jesus gave in these events. For example, in the parable of the great supper, when the guests didn't come, the master of the house told his servant to go to the highways and hedges and "compel" them to come in. The shepherd went out to find the lost sheep. When the woman found the coin that was lost, she went to tell her neighbors. The prodigal son went to a far country; but when he came to himself, he returned to his father. The rich man went to Hades, but Lazarus the beggar was carried to Abraham's bosom by the angels. Jesus told Lazarus to "come forth" from the grave. The lepers were to "go to the temple"; the blind man was to "go his way"; Zacchaeus was to "come down."

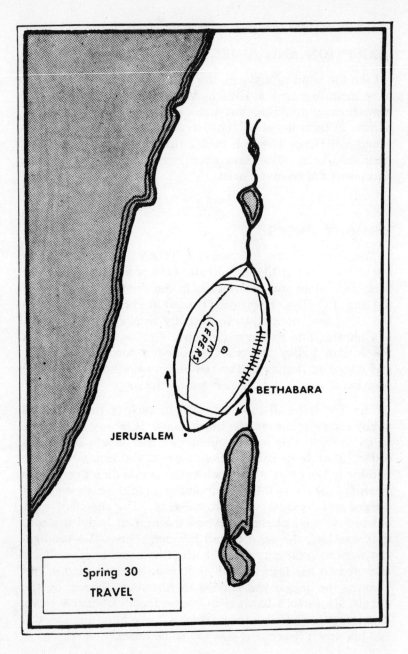

TO
LEPERS

• BETHABARA

JERUSALEM •

Spring 30
TRAVEL

THREE RESTORATIONS FROM THE DEAD

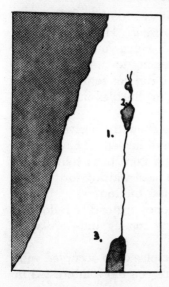

During His ministry Jesus raised three people from the dead.

1. The widow's son in S-28 (Nain). His body was being taken to the graveyard.
2. Jairus' daughter in F-28 (Capernaum). She had just died.
3. Lazarus in SP-30 (Bethany). He had been dead four days.

These restorations occurred at different times and places with people who had been dead for different lengths of time. They were not fake miracles performed at some "sacred site."

WHAT GOD IS LIKE

His faithfulness: Jesus determined to go to the cross to provide salvation and to fulfill all the Old Testament prophecy.

His tenderness and love: Jesus blessed the little children.

His grace (Matt. 20:7), *His justice* (Matt. 20:2, 10, 13), and *His sovereignty* (Matt. 20:1-16): These are all illustrated in the parable of the laborers in the vineyard.

His knowledge: Jesus' knowledge of things beyond this world was revealed as He disclosed what happened after the deaths of Lazarus and the rich man.

His power: Jesus healed the sick and restored the dead to life. He was able to cause Lazarus' body that was bound with graveclothes to come forth out of the tomb without help.

121

QUESTIONS FOR MEDITATION

1. Lazarus' sisters thought that it was too late. They had no hope that Jesus could help them. Have you classified certain people as hopeless? Have you quit praying for them? Do you avoid witnessing to them?

2. Nine lepers whom Jesus healed did not return to thank Him. Have you been thankful for the blessings God has given you?

3. Jesus told the ten lepers to go show themselves to the priest. As they went, they were healed. They left in faith, believing Christ. Has the Lord been telling you to do something but you have been waiting for "signs" to occur to prove the faithfulness of God?

4. The rich young ruler chose money instead of following Christ. Have you been letting money interfere with your service for Him?

5. James, John and the other disciples were occupied with thoughts of high positions. Are you more interested in high positions and the honors of men than you are in proclaiming the message of the cross?

CHAPTER 15

TRIUMPHAL ENTRY

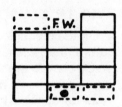

SUNDAY OF JESUS' FINAL WEEK, SPRING OF A.D. 30

KEY WORD: F.W.

Key Events of Final Week	Matthew	Mark	Luke	John
Sunday—Triumphal entry	21:1-11	11:1-11	19:29-44	12:12-19
Monday—Second cleansing of the temple	21:12-22	11:12-26	19:45-48	12:20-50
Tuesday—Jesus challenged, Olivet discourse	21:23—26:16	11:27—14:11	20:1—22:6	
Wednesday—				
Thursday—Passover supper, upper room discourse, Gethsemane arrest	26:17-56	14:12-52	22:7-53	13:1—18:12
Friday—Trial, crucifixion, burial	26:57—27:66	14:53—15:47	22:54—23:56	18:12—19:42
Saturday—In the tomb				

Over one-fourth of the content of the Gospels is used to record the final week of Christ's earthly ministry. You will study each day separately.

SUNDAY

Key Events	Matthew	Mark	Luke	John
1. Disciples sent for colt	21:1-7	11:1-7	19:29-35	12:12-16
2. Triumphal entry	21:8-9	11:8-10	19:36-44	12:17-19
3. In Jerusalem and in the temple	21:10-11, 14-17	11:11		

123

Read at least the fullest account of each event.
See the map of Jerusalem in Appendix G.

THE TRIUMPHAL ENTRY OF MESSIAH

On the first day of the week Jesus left Bethany and started toward Jerusalem. As He came near Bethphage by the Mount of Olives, He sent two of His disciples ahead for a colt that had never been ridden. A great multitude of people had come to the Feast of Passover. When they heard that Jesus was coming to Jerusalem, they took palm branches and went forth to meet Him (John 12:12-13). There were among the multitude those who had been with Jesus when He had raised Lazarus from the dead. This was another reason the multitude wanted to see Jesus: He had raised the dead.

THE KING CAME ACCORDING TO PROPHECY

He came riding "a colt the foal of an ass" (Matt. 21:4-5) that the Scriptures might be fulfilled (Zech. 9:9). As He came, the people shouted, "Hosanna," which in the Hebrew means "Save, we pray." "And they that went before, and they that followed, cried, saying, Hosanna; Blessed is he that cometh in the name of the Lord: Blessed be the kingdom of our father David, that cometh in the name of the Lord: Hosanna in the highest" (Mark 11:9-10).

This made the Pharisees very angry; and they said among themselves, "Perceive ye how ye prevail nothing? behold, the world is gone after him" (John 12:19). Some of them told the Lord to rebuke His disciples; but He told them that if the disciples were silent, the very stones would cry out.

JERUSALEM SHAKEN

When Jesus came to Jerusalem, all the city was moved (Matt. 21:10). The word *moved* in Greek literally means "shaken as by an earthquake." The multitude with Him said, "This is Jesus the prophet of Nazareth of Galilee." When the blind and the lame heard that Jesus was there, they came to Him, and He healed them. The chief priests and scribes saw Him perform these miracles; but they were indignant when the children in the temple kept saying, "Hosanna to the son of David" (Matt. 21:14-16). Jesus did not stay all night in Jerusalem but returned to Bethany with the twelve.

WHAT GOD IS LIKE

His omniscience: Jesus told the disciples exactly where to find the colt.

His compassion: He cried over the city of Jerusalem because they were rejecting Him, their promised Messiah.

JESUS THE PERFECT MAN

Jesus, even according to prophecy, came in meekness (Zech. 9:9). His life and words brought praise to God (Luke 19:37). Jesus showed His knowledge of the Scriptures when the chief priests and scribes criticized Him for not reproving the people who were crying, "Hosanna to the son of David." Jesus referred to Scripture. He said that out of the mouth of babes God had perfected praise (see Ps. 8:2).

QUESTIONS FOR MEDITATION

1. As Jesus came fulfilling prophecy, the people praised God because of His mighty works. Do your actions today cause people to praise God?
2. Jesus knew where the colt was. Do you think He can help you find the answers to your problems?
3. Jesus knew the Scriptures. Are you familiar enough with the Scriptures so that the Holy Spirit can use them to guide you or to give you understanding so that you can meet the problems of this day?

CHAPTER 16

TEMPLE CLEANSED

MONDAY

Key Events	Matthew	Mark	Luke	John
1. Cursing of fig tree	21:18-19	11:12-14		
2. Second cleansing of the temple	21:12-13	11:15-18	19:45-48	
3. Desire of Greeks to see Jesus				12:20-26
4. Voice from heaven				12:27-50

Read at least the fullest account of each event.

CURSING OF FIG TREE

On the way to Jerusalem Jesus saw a fig tree; but when He went to it, it had leaves but no fruit. Jesus pronounced a curse on it. The fig is used in the Old Testament to symbolize national Israel (see Hosea 9:10; Joel 1:7). National Israel, instead of bringing forth fruit and believing the Messiah, was rejecting Him. He told that generation, "If ye believe not that I am he, ye shall die in your sins" (John 8:24).

SECOND CLEANSING OF THE TEMPLE

In the summer of 27, at the beginning of His ministry, Jesus had cleansed the temple. Now He entered it again and cast out them that bought and sold, and overturned the tables of the money changers and the seats of them that sold the doves. He said,

"Ye have made it a den of thieves" (Mark 11:17). This made the chief priests, the scribes, and the chief of the people very angry. They tried to find a way to destroy Jesus, but they were afraid of the multitudes who listened very attentively to His teaching.

JESUS FORETOLD HIS COMING DEATH

Jesus knew that the time for His death was rapidly approaching. He said, "The hour is come, that the Son of man should be glorified" (John 12:23). Although Jesus was God, He also was man and expressed very human feelings: "Now is my soul troubled; and what shall I say? Father, save me from this hour: but for this cause came I unto this hour. Father, glorify thy name" (John 12:27-28). The Father answered Him with a voice from heaven: "I have both glorified it, and will glorify it again" (v. 28). Jesus knew how He would die, that it would not be by stoning or strangling but by crucifixion: "And I, if I be lifted up from the earth, will draw all men unto me. This he said, signifying what death he should die" (John 12:32-33).

The response of the crowd to this voice from heaven was divided. Some said, "It thundered." Others said, "An angel spake to him" (compare Acts 9:3-7).

RECEPTION AND REJECTION OF CHRIST

"But though he had done so many miracles before them, yet they believed not on him" (John 12:37). The religious rulers and leaders of the people actively plotted to kill Jesus, but not all of them. "Nevertheless among the chief rulers also many believed on him; but because of the Pharisees they did not confess him, lest they should be put out of the synagogue: for they loved the praise of men more than the praise of God" (John 12:42-43).

Those who rejected Jesus Christ will be judged by His

word: "He that rejecteth me, and receiveth not my words, hath one that judgeth him: the word that I have spoken, the same shall judge him in the last day" (John 12:48).

JESUS THE PERFECT MAN

As the perfect Man, Jesus spoke only what the Father told Him (John 12:50). As a perfect man He showed His courage as He cleansed the temple. He stood against the religious hierarchy of Judaism and told them how they had changed the house of prayer into a den of thieves. Jesus knew that He was facing the cross. Humanly speaking, He shrank from the ordeal that lay before Him. He asked, "What shall I say? Father, save me from this hour: but for this cause came I unto this hour" (John 12:27). Jesus answered His own question and obediently submitted Himself to the task that lay before Him by saying, "Father, glorify thy name" (John 12:28).

WHAT GOD IS LIKE

His power to judge: As He performed the miracle of the withered fig tree, Jesus demonstrated His power to judge and His power over nature.

His wrath: Jesus showed His wrath as He cleansed the temple. The Jews had perverted the very heart of the worship set up by God. The details that should have pointed to Jesus the Saviour were being misused by the religious leaders for personal profit.

His knowledge of the future: Jesus foretold details concerning His death: (1) the manner of His death—"lifted up"; (2) the judgment of this world (world system); (3) Satan, the prince of the world, would be cast out; (4) Christ's death would be the means whereby He would draw all men to Himself.

THE PERSONALITIES OF THE GODHEAD

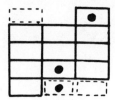

The personalities of the God-head were shown when the Father, with a voice from heaven, spoke to the Son. This was the third time that this happened in the ministry of the Lord. The first time, at His baptism (F-26), all three Persons of the Godhead were revealed. The second time, at the transfiguration (S-29), the Father spoke to the Son. This third time, during the final week, the Father's voice again was heard.

QUESTIONS FOR MEDITATION

1. There were several believers among the rulers, but they kept silent, for they loved the praise of men more than the praise of God. Has your failure to witness or to take a stand for Jesus Christ been because you loved the praise of men more than the praise of God?

2. Jesus said, "If any man serve me, let him follow me; and where I am, there shall also my servant be: if any man serve me, him will my Father honour" (John 12:26). This, stated in a different order, teaches that you cannot serve the Lord unless you are following Him. Have you learned this secret of service?

CHAPTER 17

DAY OF CONTROVERSY

TUESDAY

Key Events	Matthew	Mark	Luke
1. Jesus challenged concerning authority	21:23-27	11:27-33	20:1-8
2. Parables of rejection:			
The two sons	21:28-32		
Parable of the vineyard	21:33-46	12:1-12	20:9-19
The marriage feast and the wedding garment	22:1-14		
3. Attempts to trap or discredit Jesus:			
Question about tribute to Caesar	22:15-22	12:13-17	20:20-26
Question about resurrection	22:23-33	12:18-27	20:27-40
Question about greatest commandment	22:34-40	12:28-34	
Jesus denounces scribes and Pharisees	22:41—23:39	12:35-44	20:41—21:4
4. Olivet discourse:			
Destruction of Jerusalem, signs of the second coming, signs of the end of the age	24:1-31	13:1-27	21:5-28
Parable of the fig tree	24:32-41	13:28-32	21:29-33
Parables teaching readiness	24:42—25:13	13:33-37	21:34-36
Parables of judgment	25:14-46		
Jesus predicts His death	26:1-2		
5. Enemies plot against Jesus:			
The religious leaders	26:3-5	14:1-2	22:1-2
Judas	26:14-16	14:10-11	22:3-6

Read at least the fullest account of each event.

A DAY OF CHALLENGE

Tuesday of the final week was a day in which Jesus silenced His critics. The first group that came to Him in the court of the temple were the chief priests, the scribes and the elders. They challenged His authority for the things that He had been doing. Their hearts were hardened; for almost two years they had been accusing Him of using evil powers. They wouldn't have believed Jesus if He had told them that His authority was the authority of God, so He asked them a question. He said, if they answered it, He would answer their question. He asked whether the ministry of John the Baptist was from heaven or from men. The Jews would not answer because they knew that if they said, "From heaven," Jesus would ask them why they did not believe what John said. If they said, "From men," they were afraid of what the people would do to them because the people considered John a prophet.

PARABLES OF REJECTION

When they wouldn't answer His question, Jesus warned them by three parables: the two sons, the wicked husbandman, and the marriage of the king's son.

In His parables of rejection, Jesus taught the following:

1. Many will reject the King: the self-righteous (scribes, Pharisees, religious rulers, and the proud).

2. Some will receive Him: those who realize that they are sinners (publicans, harlots, common people, and some rulers).

3. The King, the Son of God, will be killed.

4. The rejecting generation will be judged.

5. The kingdom will be given to another generation that will receive the King. (The Bible does not teach that God will break His promise to Israel by giving the kingdom to another [Gentile nations]; and it does *not* teach that the

kingdom has been given to the church. It will be given to another generation that receives Jesus at His second coming).

When the chief priests and the Pharisees understood that these parables were talking about them, they tried to take Jesus; but they were afraid to do so because of the multitude.

THE HERODIANS AND THE PHARISEES TRIED TO TRAP JESUS

The Pharisees formed an unusual alliance with the Herodians, a political party that wanted to restore the Herodian family rule over Judaea. Pharisees and Herodians were normally bitter enemies. They asked Jesus a question: "Is it lawful for us to give tribute unto Caesar, or no?" (Luke 20:22). If He said, "No," He would be in trouble with Rome. If He said, "Yes," He would be in trouble with the people because they did not like being ruled by Rome. He requested a penny and asked them whose inscription was on it. When they answered, "Caesar's," He said, "Render therefore unto Caesar the things which be Caesar's, and unto God the things which be God's" (Luke 20:25).

THE SADDUCEES ASKED ABOUT THE RESURRECTION

Next the Sadducees came to Jesus. They did not believe in the supernatural nor in a resurrection. Yet they tried to discredit Him with a supposed problem of one woman who married seven brothers in turn (see Gen. 38:8; Deut. 25:5-6). "In the resurrection," they asked, "whose wife will she be?" Jesus told them that they didn't understand that when people are raised there will be no more marrying or giving in marriage, but they will be as the angels. By this He did not mean that they would look like angels or become angels.

132

This is a figure of speech, a simile. He was comparing angels and those who are resurrected in one special respect. Each angel is a separate creation. Angels do not marry or have offspring. In the resurrection, people will not have the normal marriage relationship that they have here on earth nor will they have children born to them. The Sadducees tried to discredit Jesus on an intellectual basis—inferring that He was teaching things that were unreasonable and inconsistent.

A SCRIBE QUESTIONED JESUS

A scribe asked Jesus a question: "Master, which is the great commandment in the law?" (Matt. 22:36). This was a question over which the rabbis often disputed. It seems the scribe attempted to trap Jesus in the manifold arguments of the traditional oral law. (Someone has counted the commandments given in the Old Testament and has come up with 248 positive commands and 365 negative commands.) Jesus wisely answered, "Thou shalt love the Lord thy God with all thy heart, and with all thy soul, and with all thy mind. This is the first and great commandment. And the second is like unto it, Thou shalt love thy neighbour as thyself" (Matt. 22:37-39). The scribe discreetly agreed with Jesus; and Jesus said to him, "Thou art not far from the kingdom of God." And no man after that dared ask Him any questions (Mark 12:34).

CHRIST'S UNANSWERABLE QUESTION

Jesus then asked the Pharisees a question: "What think ye of Christ? whose son is he?" They answered Him, "The son of David." Jesus then asked, "How then doth David in spirit call him Lord, saying, The LORD said unto my Lord, Sit thou on my right hand, till I make thine enemies thy footstool? If David then call him Lord, how is he his son?" And no man was able to answer Him a word, neither dared any man from that day forth ask Him any more questions (Matt. 22:43-46).

133

JESUS WARNED THE PEOPLE

Jesus warned His disciples and the multitude to "beware of the scribes." He said that they (1) bound heavy burdens on the people, (2) did their works to be seen of men, (3) wore their clothes in such a fashion as to appear pious, (4) loved the chief places at the feasts, (5) loved to be called rabbi or teacher, (6) devoured widow's houses, (7) made a pretense with long prayers, and (8) went anywhere and did anything in order to make a proselyte (convert one to their teaching).

Jesus' big indictment of the scribes was that through their teaching and manner of living they prevented people from understanding how to be saved. Jesus called them hypocrites and blind guides.

In contrast to this hypocritical practice of religion, Jesus pointed out a woman who had brought two mites to the temple treasury. He said, "She cast in more than all these because she gave all that she had."

THE UNFOLDING REVELATION ABOUT THE KINGDOM

In the Old Testament God promised the kingdom to Israel. In the New Testament we see its development.

1. John the Baptist first preached that the kingdom of God was at hand (Luke 16:16). Then Jesus and His disciples also proclaimed it.

2. The kingdom of heaven parables were given after the religious leaders of Israel rejected the King. They revealed three main things: (1) The kingdom will be set up after a period of time. (2) Evil workers will continue to oppose it during the present age. (3) There will be a judgment at the end of the age. It will help you to keep the kingdom of heaven parables in their proper perspective if you will substitute the words "unrevealed truth" for "mystery" and then

read Luke 8:10: "Unto you it is given to know the unrevealed truth of the kingdom of God."

3. The parables of rejection gave details of the rejection of the King.

4. In the Olivet discourse Jesus gave details concerning Israel and world conditions from the rejection of the King to His second coming.

OLIVET DISCOURSE

Jesus and His disciples went by the temple. He told them that it would be destroyed. This caused them to ask three questions: (1) When will be the destruction of Jerusalem? (2) When will be the sign of His coming? (3) When will be the sign of the end of the world (age)?

Jesus began His Olivet discourse by warning them that many would try to lead them astray (Matt. 24:4-5). He gave a whole list of things that would happen, unusual events that might be thought of as signs: wars and rumors of wars, famines, earthquakes, pestilences, fearful sights, great signs from heaven, persecution of His followers, division among families, false prophets, iniquity abounding, love of many waxing cold, and the gospel of the kingdom being preached in the whole world. Then the end of the age would come.

The book of Revelation gives many additional details for this period of time. For example, the gospel will be preached during this period of tribulation by 144,000 Jewish witnesses (Rev. 7:4-8; 14:1-5). The wars, plagues, and other signs are described more fully starting in chapter 6.

Matthew 24:13 says, "But he that shall endure unto the end, the same shall be saved." This needs to be studied in context. If you read Matthew 24:4-13, you will see that after describing perilous times in which many will die, the promise is given that if the people endure to the end they shall be saved from physical death. This is not teaching that you must endure and be faithful until you die, and then you will be saved eternally. Salvation is always by grace through faith (Eph. 2:8-9). In this case the word *saved* isn't speak-

135

ing about eternal salvation. Paul also used the word *saved* in Acts 27:31 in the sense of being spared from physical death.

THE SIGN OF THE DESTRUCTION OF JERUSALEM

In A.D. 70 Jerusalem was destroyed by the armies of Rome, but the Scriptures seem to teach that there will be another destruction of Jerusalem at the end of the age. It seems like the account in Luke 21:20-21 is speaking specifically about the first destruction of Jerusalem which foreshadows the destruction in the end time. Matthew 24:15 gives a definite sign of the second destruction of Jerusalem, "the abomination of desolation" spoken of by Daniel the prophet (Dan. 9:27; 11:31; 12:11).

PARABLE OF THE FIG TREE

Jesus taught in the parable of the fig tree that the generation that sees these signs will be able to know it is the season when these things shall come to pass, but that they will not be able to know the exact time. He will come suddenly and the world will not expect Him, even as it was in the days of Noah.

PARABLES OF READINESS

Jesus gave a series of parables teaching His disciples that they were to be ready for His second coming: the porter, the master of the house, the faithful and the evil servant, and the ten virgins. He said that neither the angels nor the Son, humanly speaking, but only the Father knew the time that the Son would return.

PARABLES OF JUDGMENT

Jesus told the parable of the talents, in which He taught His disciples to be faithful because they were accountable. The talents were divided among the servants, "to every man according to his several abilities." In the parable He em-

136

phasized the fact that, after a long time, the lord of the servants returned. The faithful servants were rewarded; but the slothful servants suffered loss.

PARABLE OF THE SHEEP AND THE GOATS

This parable teaches that the world will also be judged at the return of Christ as He sets up His kingdom. The basis of judgment will be what they did to His "brethren" (Matt. 25:40). At the conclusion of His Olivet discourse, the Lord reminded His disciples that in two days He would be delivered up and crucified.

FINAL PLOT AGAINST JESUS

The chief priests, the scribes, and the elders of the people (Sanhedrin) all met in the court of the High Priest Caiaphas and took counsel together how they might take Jesus with subtlety and kill Him. They were afraid of the people and didn't want to do it during the feast.

JUDAS' BARGAIN

One of the disciples, Judas Iscariot, went to the chief priests and asked them how much they were willing to pay him to deliver Christ to them. They offered him thirty pieces of silver—the price of a slave. This had been foretold in prophecy (Zech. 11:12). Judas agreed, and from that time he sought to deliver Jesus to them in the absence of the multitude (Luke 22:6).

WHAT GOD IS LIKE

His omniscience: Christ told in detail about His rejection, His crucifixion, the order of events to come, and the eternal conditions in the resurrection.

His justice: The parables of judgment revealed His justice as He dealt with His disciples and His enemies, and as He commended a poor widow who gave her all—the two mites.

137

RECEPTION AND REJECTION OF CHRIST

By Tuesday the rejection of Christ had almost reached a climax. The traitor had been hired to deliver Jesus into the hands of His enemies at a time when the multitude would not interfere.

QUESTIONS FOR MEDITATION

1. Jesus taught His disciples that the proper attitude for a disciple was to live in readiness and to be watching for His return. Is this your attitude? Would you be ready if Jesus came today?
2. Judas sold out the Saviour for thirty pieces of silver. Christians sometimes betray Him for much less. How faithful are you? What does it take to cause you to desert Him? A favorite TV program? A boat on the lake? An extra hour of sleep?

WEDNESDAY—NO RECORDED EVENTS

Following the traditional schedule of the Friday crucifixion, there are no events recorded for Wednesday.

See Appendixes R, Q and Z.

CHAPTER 18

UPPER ROOM DISCOURSE

THURSDAY

Key Events	Matthew	Mark	Luke	John
1. Preparation for the Passover:	26:17-19	14:12-17	22:7-13	
Disciples' feet washed by Jesus				13:1-20
Passover supper	26:21-25	14:18-21	22:14-23	13:21-30
Peter's denial foretold	26:31-35	14:27-31	22:31-38	13:31-38
2. The Lord's Supper (I Cor. 11:23-26)	26:26-29	14:22-25	22:17-20	
3. Upper room discourse: Christ's second coming				14:1-15
Promise of the Holy Spirit				14:16-31
Vine and the branches				15:1-27
Work of the Holy Spirit				16:1-33
Jesus' prayer of intercession				17:1-26
4. Gethsemane	26:30-46	14:26-42	22:39-46	18:1
5. Arrest of Jesus	26:47-56	14:43-52	22:47-53	18:2-12

Read at least the fullest account of each event.

PREPARATION FOR THE PASSOVER

Jesus sent His disciples on ahead to an upper room that was prepared for them to observe the Passover. They were to go into the city and meet a man carrying a pitcher. By this sign they would know that they were to tell him that the Master and His disciples wanted to use his guest room.

139

Jesus, the Lamb of God, who is our Passover (I Cor. 5:7) told His disciples, "With [great] desire I have desired to eat this Passover with you before I suffer" (Luke 22:15). When you consider the disciples as being the most faithful of all Jesus' followers, and His followers as being among the best living representatives of the human race, a paradox is evident as you consider the grace of God shown to those with whom Jesus partook of the Passover:

1. *The betrayer*—Judas (Luke 22:21).

2. *The self-seekers*—Some of the disciples were arguing among themselves as to who should be the greatest (Luke 22:24).

3. *The forsakers*—When Jesus was arrested, the disciples all scattered and forsook Him (Matt. 26:56; Mark 14:27).

4. *The denier and curser*—Peter denied and cursed his Lord (Luke 22:34).

5. *The sleepers*—In Gethsemane when Jesus prayed, His disciples slept (Luke 22:45).

Nevertheless Jesus promised them a place in His kingdom, judging the twelve tribes of Israel (Luke 22:29).

JESUS WASHED HIS DISCIPLES FEET

The upper room was all prepared for the Passover, but there were no servants to wash their feet. It was unthinkable that any of the disciples would stoop to do this—they were arguing about who was the greatest—so Jesus washed their feet. He used this incident to explain His work on the cross and the forgiveness of sin (see I John 1:9). He told them that He had given them an example and they ought to do as He had done. Some Christians understand this to mean that Christians should wash one another's feet as an ordinance in the church. There is no record in the book of Acts or the epistles that the disciples ever practiced foot washing as an ordinance. If it is done with the proper attitude, it could be very meaningful to the people who participate in it; but it seems that the disciples understood it to mean that they should in humility have a spiritual ministry one to another.

THE PASSOVER SUPPER

While they were eating, Jesus said that one of them would betray Him. The disciples wondered who Jesus meant. Jesus indicated that the one to whom He gave the sop was the one who would betray Him. He gave it to Judas.

SATAN ENTERS JUDAS

He then told Judas, "That thou doest, do quickly" (John 13:27). Judas left, and Jesus then warned His disciples about the events that were ahead and foretold that Peter would deny Him three times before the cock crowed.

THE LORD'S SUPPER

The Old Testament sacrificial system instituted by God was about to be fulfilled. The offerings demonstrated, explained and foretold the work of Christ on the cross. In the Old Testament, God had promised a New Covenant (see Jer. 31:31-34; Ezek. 37:26-28; Isa. 61). The New Covenant was specifically promised to the nation of Israel. Some feel that there is a twofold application of this New Covenant—first of all to the Jews in their future kingdom and at the present time to the church. There is a similarity between the blessings on Christians today and the promises made in the New Covenant to Israel.

Other Bible students feel that there are two new covenants mentioned in Scripture. The first one was promised to Israel in the Old Testament, and the second one given in the New Testament to the church. Those who hold this view consider I Corinthians 11:23-26 and Hebrews 8:6; 9:15; 10:29; 13:20 as referring to the New Covenant made with Israel. (The word translated "testament" as used in Hebrews 9:15 is the same word that is translated "covenant" in Hebrews 8:8 and other places.)

The Lord Jesus Christ instituted the Lord's Supper as a memorial observance wherever believers gather in His name. The bread is to be a reminder that He became flesh and lived

141

among men and that His body was broken for them. The cup symbolizes His blood shed on Calvary's cross for the sin of man. "For as often as ye eat this bread, and drink this cup, ye do show the Lord's death till he come" (I Cor. 11:26). The Lord's Supper' itself has in no way a magical power. It is to be observed for a specific length of time: "till he come." Jesus said that He would not again partake of the fruit of the vine until He partakes of it in the kingdom (Mark 14:25; Matt. 26:29; Luke 22:18).

THE SECOND COMING OF CHRIST FOR HIS OWN

Jesus emphasized another truth, repeating it many times that night: He was going away; He was about to return to His Father (John 13:1; 14:2, 28; 16:5, 7, 16, 28; 17:13).

Up until this time Jesus had just announced that He was going to build a church—a called-out assembly (Matt. 16:18). The disciples still did not understand its nature or mission. John 14:2-3 was the first promise that Jesus would return for the church to receive it to Himself. Further details were given later in I Thessalonians 4:13-18 and I Corinthians 15:51-53.

UPPER ROOM DISCOURSE—FOUNDATIONAL CHURCH TRUTH

John 14–17 is commonly called the upper room discourse. Jesus began this discourse in the upper room and evidently finished it as He and His disciples were walking to Gethsemane.

PROGRESSIVE REVELATION OF THE CHURCH

Jesus came as the King of Israel, offering the kingdom to the nation; but the nation did not receive Him as King. In the summer of A.D. 29, Jesus first told of His church or called-out assembly. After Peter's good confession, He said, "On this rock I will build my church." The word *church* in the original language can literally be translated "a calling out." It was used in secular society to describe a body of citizens gathered to discuss affairs of state (Acts 19:39). This was the first indication that, out of the rejecting of Israel, God was going to "call out" an assembly, or a group of people who would believe on Him. He told them later that Gentiles would also be in His assembly (Acts 1:8; Eph. 2:11-16). Jesus said, "I have yet many things to say unto you, but ye cannot bear them now" (John 16:12). He promised, "When he, the Spirit of truth, is come, he will guide you into all truth" (John 16:13) "and bring all things to your remembrance, whatsoever I have said unto you" (John 14:26). The full explanation of the church came much later (Eph. 3:2-6).

THE REVELATION OF GOD IN CHRIST JESUS

When Philip said to Jesus, "Lord, shew us the Father," Jesus said to him, "Have I been so long time with you, and yet hast thou not known me, Philip? he that hath seen me hath seen the Father" (John 14:8-9). "God was manifest [revealed] in the flesh" (I Tim. 3:16; John 1:14). God took on human flesh, walked about this earth, and revealed to man what He was like. Now Jesus revealed the first hint of the mission of the church which was later explained in Colossians 1:26-27: "Even the mystery [unrevealed truth] which hath been hid from ages and from generations, but now is made manifest to his saints: to whom God would make known what is the riches of the glory of this mystery among the Gentiles; which is Christ in you, the hope of glory." God is calling out a group of people that will form a new body for Him. At the most, Jesus as the God-man could minister or talk to only several thousand at one time. If Jesus, after His resurrection, had gone to India and spent one day in each village, even today in the twentieth century He still would not have covered every village. In His new body, the church, He will minister to millions. It will not be just to one nation (Israel) but to all nations (the Gentiles).

143

GREATER WORKS

Jesus said, "He that believeth on me, the works that I do shall he do also; and greater works than these shall he do" (John 14:12). Jesus through His new body, the church, will perform miracles like the ones He performed in His earthly ministry. He will heal the sick, cast out demons, and raise the dead; and He will proclaim the good news of salvation to untold millions (Acts 2:5; 3:2-8; 5:12; 9:36-41; 13:2-3; 15:14-17; 16:16-18; 17:30-31; 19:11-17; 26:14-18; 28:28).

THE PROVISION FOR SERVICE

Jesus promised His followers the privilege of praying in His name and that He will answer (John 14:13-14). He also promised "another Comforter." The word translated "another" means "another of the same kind." The word translated "Comforter" means "one called alongside to help." In an expanded translation, John 14:16 would be translated, "And I will pray the Father, and he shall give you another Comforter, just like me, who will be alongside to help you, that he may abide with you forever." Through the ministry of the Holy Spirit the disciples would be taught other things later. The Holy Spirit would bring to their remembrance the things that Jesus had taught them (John 14:26; 16:13). Jesus promised His disciples that the Holy Spirit would abide with them, and be in them forever, and that He and the Father would come and "make our abode with him" (John 14:16-17, 23).

THE PRINCIPLE OF FRUIT-BEARING

Jesus explained that in order to bear fruit for Him, His followers must abide in fellowship with Him by being obedient (John 14:21; 15:10). He clearly explained that there is no such thing as fruit-bearing through self-effort. "For without me ye can do nothing" (see John 15:4-5). The Lord expects His followers to be fruitful, and He expects that their fruit will remain (John 15:16).

THE MINISTRY OF THE HOLY SPIRIT TO THE WORLD

The Holy Spirit will "reprove the world of sin, and of righteousness, and of judgment: of sin, because they believe not on me; of righteousness, because I go to my Father, and ye see me no more; of judgment, because the prince of this world is judged" (John 16:8-11).

JESUS' HIGH PRIESTLY PRAYER

In John 17 Jesus prayed for His own. He prayed for their safe keeping (v. 11), that they might have joy (v. 13), that they be kept from evil (v. 15), for their sanctification (v. 17), for their unity (v. 21), for their glorification (v. 22), for their presence in heaven with Him (v. 24), and that His love might be in them (v. 26). He did not pray only for those disciples that were there with Him but "for them also which shall believe on me through their word" (John 17:20).

GETHSEMANE

Jesus went with His disciples into the garden of Gethsemane, which is located on the Mount of Olives, to pray. He took Peter, James and John with Him a little farther and told them to watch. Then He fell on His face and prayed. As God, He understood the terrible experience that lay before Him. As man, He was very sorrowful and troubled: "Father, if thou be willing, remove this cup from me. Nevertheless, not my will but thine be done." As the perfect man, Jesus subjected His will to the Father's. His followers were tired and went to sleep. He came back to them and asked them to watch and pray but again they went to sleep. When He came to them the third time, He told them that the hour was at hand and that He, the Son of man, was about to be betrayed.

THE ARREST

Judas knew the place where Jesus often went to pray, and

145

he brought a band of men and officers from the chief priests as well as some of the high priest's servants (John 18:3, 10, 12). The word translated "band" is the word for six hundred Roman soldiers. The officers from the chief priests were probably the Jewish temple guard. There also were some of the chief priests, captains of the temple, and elders or members of the Sanhedrin present (Luke 22:52). Altogether this made a large group that came to take Jesus. Judas led the band to Jesus and kissed Him. This was not an unusual custom. A disciple often kissed his rabbi as a token of respect and greeting. Jesus asked whom they were seeking. They said, "Jesus of Nazareth." He replied, "I am he." As soon as He said that, they went backward, and fell to the ground (John 18:5-6). It seems as though the very power of Christ's words knocked them to the ground. Yet they were not to be denied their evil works. As they came forward, Peter drew his sword and cut off the ear of the high priest's servant. Right before their eyes Jesus performed His last miracle before going to the cross, as He healed the ear of the servant. Yet this seemingly had no effect on the group that had come to take Him. Jesus told His disciples that if He wanted to He could send for more than twelve legions of angels; but then the Scriptures could not have been fulfilled, for He came into the world to die for the sins of all mankind. Then Jesus said to the chief priests, the captains of the temple, and the elders which had come to Him, "Be ye come out, as against a thief, with swords and staves? When I was daily with you in the temple, ye stretched forth no hands against me: but this is your hour, and the power of darkness" (Luke 22:52-53). Taking Jesus, they bound Him and led Him to the high priest.

JESUS THE PERFECT MAN

Jesus as the perfect Man showed His humility as He washed the feet of the disciples (John 13:14). He enjoyed fellowship during the Passover meal, and He desired prayer fellowship as He prayed in the garden. Jesus spent much time in prayer. Communion with the Father was very important to Him. When He was arrested, He thought of others and asked that His disciples be allowed to go free (John 18:8).

WHAT GOD IS LIKE

His knowledge: Jesus foretold many details of the events that lay before Him: His betrayal, His denial by Peter, His death, His resurrection, and His second coming.

QUESTIONS FOR MEDITATION

1. Jesus placed a great value upon the fellowship He had with His disciples. What value do you place upon the time you spend in fellowship with other Christians? With Him?
2. Jesus said that without Him you can do nothing. In your Christian service, do you really believe this? Or do you just ask the Lord's help for "big" things and try to do the "little" things by yourself?
3. Jesus prayed for the safety of His followers (John 17:11, 24). Do you realize the completeness of salvation in Christ?
4. Jesus prayed that there might be purity, unity, joy and love among His followers. Are these the things that characterize your life?

See Appendixes S and T.

147

CHAPTER 19

THE CROSS

FRIDAY

Key Events	Matthew	Mark	Luke	John
1. Jesus' trials:				
Before Annas				18:12-14, 19-23
Before Caiaphas	26:57-68	14:53-65	22:54, 63-65	18:24
Before the Sanhedrin	27:1	15:1	22:66-71	
Before Pilate (1)	27:2, 11-14	15:1-5	23:1-5	18:28-38
Before Herod			23:6-12	
Before Pilate (2)	27:15-30	15:6-19	23:13-25	18:39— 19:16
2. Peter's denial of his Lord	26:58, 69-75	14:54, 66-72	22:54-62	18:15-18, 25-27
3. The suicide of Judas (Acts 1:18-19)	27:3-10			
4. The crucifixion:				
On the way to the cross	27:31-34	15:20-23	23:26-33	19:16-17
The first three hours on the cross	27:35-44	15:24-32	23:33-43	19:18-27
Three hours of darkness	27:45-50	15:33-37	23:44-46	19:28-30
Signs accompanying His death	27:51-56	15:38-41	23:45, 47-49	
5. The burial of Jesus	27:57-66	15:42-47	23:50-56	19:31-42

Read at least the fullest account of each event.

THE FIRST TRIAL

Jesus' trials can be divided into two sections. The first three were religious trials; the last three were civil trials. He was brought first before Annas, the deposed high priest. There was no formal indictment. They asked Jesus concerning His disciples and His teaching. He replied that He had taught openly in the synagogues and in the temple. He said they could ask those who had heard Him. One of the officers standing nearby struck Jesus with his hand. This was the first of much physical abuse that Jesus received during His trials.

THE SECOND TRIAL

They led Jesus away to the house of Caiaphas the high priest where many of the chief priests, elders (members of the Sandhedrin), and scribes were assembled. They brought many false witnesses to try to accuse Him of something worthy of death, but they couldn't agree. When the high priest asked Jesus under oath whether He was the Christ, the Son of God, Jesus answered, "Thou hast said." In the original Greek, this is a strong affirmative which means an emphatic yes. The high priest said that this was blasphemy; then they began to abuse Jesus.

THE THIRD TRIAL

In the morning the high priest convened the Sandhedrin. They again asked Him if He was Christ; but He said, "If I tell you, you will not believe." Then they asked Him, "Art thou the Son of God?" He said unto them, "Ye say that I am" (Luke 22:70). The Sanhedrin officially confirmed that He was guilty of blasphemy because He said that He was the Christ and the Son of God. But the Jews had a problem. The Romans would not allow them to pass sentences of death. The case must be reviewed by the Roman governor, so Jesus was taken before Pilate.

THE FOURTH TRIAL

When they brought Jesus before Pilate, he asked them what Jesus had done. They replied that if He were not an evildoer, they would not have brought Him to Pilate. Pilate, who had no love for the Jews, said, "Take Him and judge Him acording to your law." But the Jews had to admit that they were not allowed to put anyone to death and so they charged Jesus with three things: (1) perverting the nation, (2) forbidding to give tribute to Caesar, and (3) saying that He Himself was Christ, their King (Luke 23:2). When Pilate asked Jesus if He was the King of the Jews, He admitted that He was, but said, "My kingdom is not of this world [literally, 'does not have its origin in this world system']." If it were, Jesus' servants would have fought in order to prevent His being delivered to the Jews. Jesus came as a King, but the people He came to and offered the kingdom to—the Jewish people—rejected Him. Pilate's final decision was "Not guilty": "I find no fault in this man" (Luke 23:4).

THE FIFTH TRIAL

When Pilate heard that Jesus was a Galilean, he decided to send Him to Herod Antipas because Herod ruled over Galilee. When Jesus was brought before Herod, the Jews accused Him of many things; but He remained silent and didn't answer them. Herod was very disappointed because he wanted to see Jesus perform a miracle. When Jesus would not respond to Herod, his soldiers mocked Him and then sent Him back to Pilate.

THE SIXTH TRIAL

Pilate's wife sent word and warned him to have nothing to do with "that righteous man" because of dreams she had had. It was customary for Pilate to release one prisoner to the Jews at this time; he thought he would give the people a choice between Barabbas and Jesus. Barabbas was a mur-

150

derer and a rebel. He was wanted for insurrection. He probably belonged to the Zealot political party. Pilate knew that Jesus had been delivered up because of envy by many of the Jewish leaders (Matt. 27:18). He may have remembered Jesus' popularity during the triumphal entry; but the chief priests and elders stirred up the multitude to ask for Barabbas rather than Jesus. Pilate next had Jesus scourged, then the soldiers mocked Him with a crown of thorns and a purple robe. Pilate said again, "I find no fault in him" (John 19:4, 6). He still did not want to put Jesus to death. The Jews replied, "We have a law, and by our law he ought to die, because he made himself the Son of God" (John 19:7). When Pilate heard this, he became frightened and tried harder to release Jesus; but the Jews told him, "If thou let this man go, thou art not Caesar's friend: whosoever maketh himself a king speaketh against Caesar" (John 19:12).

THE KING REJECTED

Pilate brought Jesus before the Jews and said, "Behold your King!" But they cried out, "Away with him, away with him, crucify him." Pilate said to them, "Shall I crucify your King?" The chief priests answered, "We have no king but Caesar" (John 19:14-15). Pilate then asked for water, washed his hands, and said that he was innocent of the blood of "this righteous man." Then all the people answered, "His blood be on us, and on our children" (Matt. 27:25). Finally Pilate released Barabbas and delivered up Jesus to be crucified.

After Jesus' arrest, Peter denied his Lord three times even as Jesus had prophesied. Judas brought the money back, threw it down in the temple, and went out and committed suicide. Jesus was led outside the city to a place called Golgotha—the place of the skull. This is thought to be north of the city of Jerusalem. Because of the physical abuse He had taken, Jesus was unable to carry the cross all the way, so Simon of Cyrene was forced to carry it for Him.

151

Jesus was crucified at about 9:00 in the morning. Over His head Pilate put an inscription: "JESUS OF NAZARETH THE KING OF THE JEWS" (John 19:19).

THE SEVEN SAYINGS FROM THE CROSS

1. "Father, forgive them; for they know not what they do" (Luke 23:34). Jesus probably had the Roman soldiers specifically in mind; they had carried out their orders. But His forgiveness extends to the whole world; no crime is too terrible. All anyone must do is receive Christ as his personal Saviour, and his sins are forgiven (Eph. 1:7).

2. "Today shalt thou be with me in paradise" (Luke 23:43). Jesus told this to one of the robbers on the cross who said to Him, "Lord, remember me when thou comest into thy kingdom" (Luke 23:42).

3. "Woman, behold thy son! . . . Behold thy mother!" (John 19:26-27). Jesus committed the care of His mother to His disciple John. From 12:00 noon until 3:00 P.M. there was darkness over the face of the earth.

4. "My God, my God, why hast thou forsaken me?" (Matt. 27:46). It was at this time, while He was on the cross, that the sins of the world were placed upon Jesus. In some way which the human mind cannot understand, God the Son was separated from God the Father, and experienced spiritual death in order to pay the penalty for sin. "For the wages of sin is death; but the gift of God is eternal life through Jesus Christ our Lord" (Rom. 6:23). "For he hath made him to be sin for us, who knew no sin; that we might be made the righteousness of God in him" (II Cor. 5:21). "For Christ also hath once suffered for sins, the just for the unjust, that he might bring us to God, being put to death in the flesh, but quickened by the Spirit" (I Peter 3:18).

5. "I thirst" (John 19:28). Jesus, knowing that God's purpose was now accomplished, said, "I thirst." He was given a drink of vinegar (sour wine) and again the Scriptures were fulfilled (Ps. 69:21).

6. "It is finished" (John 19:30). Salvation had been ac-

complished. The promise, first given in Genesis 3:15 and expanded and repeated thousands of times through the ages, had been fulfilled. The way back to God had been opened (John 14:6).

7. "Father, into thy hands I commend my spirit" (Luke 23:46). Jesus the perfect Man had been "obedient unto death, even the death of the cross" (Phil. 2:8).

FOUR GROUPS OF UNBELIEVERS

Standing around the cross were four groups of unbelievers:

1. They that passed by who reviled Christ (Matt. 27:39-40).

2. The chief priests who mocked Him with the scribes and the elders (Matt. 27:41-43).

3. The robbers, or thieves, who were crucified with Him (Matt. 23:44).

4. The soldiers (John 19:23-24).

FOUR FRIENDS AT THE CROSS

Although most of Jesus' disciples had forsaken Him, there were four friends at the cross: His mother, His mother's sister, Mary Magdalene, and John the disciple.

SIGNS ACCOMPANYING CHRIST'S DEATH

1. The veil in the temple was rent (Matt. 27:51).
2. There was an earthquake (Matt. 27:51).
3. Some of the dead were raised (Matt. 27:53).
4. Darkness covered the face of the earth (Matt. 27:45).

SALVATION AT THE CROSS

1. It would appear that Simon of Cyrene, who carried the cross for Jesus, became a Christian (Mark 15:21). It is thought that his sons Alexander and Rufus are again mentioned later in the New Testament.

2. The thief on the cross at first reviled Jesus, but later he acknowledged Him as Lord and King. Jesus promised him that that very day he would be with Him in paradise.

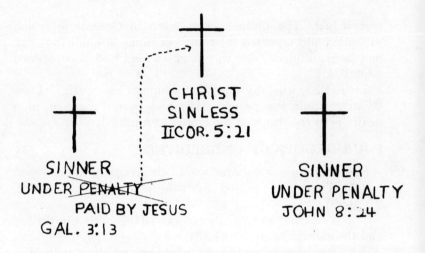

CHRIST
SINLESS
IICOR. 5:21

SINNER
UNDER ~~PENALTY~~
PAID BY JESUS
GAL. 3:13

SINNER
UNDER PENALTY
JOHN 8:24

3. The Roman centurion said after the earthquake, "Truly this was the Son of God" (Matt. 27:54).

It is at the cross that everyone has to make his decision. The cross is the great dividing line. All come before it as sinners (Rom. 3:23) under the curse of the law (Gal. 3:13; Rom. 6:23). Those who reject Jesus Christ as their Saviour will die in their sins (John 8:24) and will be judged and punished for them by eternal separation from God in torment (Rev. 20:11-15). The thief that rejected Jesus represents this group.

The repentant thief represents all those that trust in Christ as their personal Saviour. All believers' sins were judged at the cross:

Verdict: Guilty.

Penalty: Death (Christ as the believer's substitute).

Result: Penalty paid in full, sin remitted, believer justified.

"All we like sheep have gone astray; we have turned every one to his own way; and the LORD hath laid on him the iniquity of us all" (Isa. 53:6).

"Who his own self bare our sins in his own body on the

154

tree, that we, being dead to sins, should live unto righteous-ness" (I Peter 2:24).

"Verily, verily, I say unto you, He that heareth my word, and believeth on him that sent me, hath everlasting life, and shall not come into condemnation [judgment]; but is passed from death unto life" (John 5:24).

"In whom we have redemption through his blood, the for-giveness of sins, according to the riches of his grace" (Eph. 1:7).

THE BURIAL OF JESUS

Two members of the Sanhedrin, Nicodemus and Joseph of Arimathaea, tended to the burial of Jesus' body. They went to Pilate and asked permission to take it. Until this time, Joseph had been a secret disciple because of the fear of the Jews; but he is described as one who was "looking for the kingdom of God." They placed the body in Joseph's tomb which was in a garden nearby, after wrapping it with linen cloth. Nicodemus brought one hundred pounds of spices to place around Jesus' body. When they were finished, they rolled a great stone over the door. The Jews got Pilate to put a guard over the tomb and to seal it so that Jesus' disci-ples could not steal away the body and claim that He had risen. So the body of the Saviour was laid to rest.

QUESTIONS FOR MEDITATION

1. On the cross Jesus said, "It is finished." Have you ever tried to contemplate the cost of your salvation?
2. Jesus' cry "My God, my God, why hast thou forsaken me?" helps us to understand a little of the horror of the punishment for sin. Have you ever stopped to think of the horror of an eternity in torment?
3. The thief had nothing to offer and only a short time to make a decision. Perhaps your time is just as limited. Will you tell Jesus that you want Him to be your per-sonal Saviour—that you are putting your trust in Him?

See Appendixes X and Y.

CHAPTER 20

POST-RESURRECTION MINISTRY

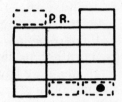

40 DAYS FOLLOWING RESURRECTION

KEY WORD: P.R.

Key Events	Matthew	Mark	Luke	John
1. Earthquake as angel rolled away stone	28:1-4			
2. Visits to tomb:				
Women visit tomb	28:5-8	16:1-8	24:1-8	20:1-2
Peter and John visit tomb			24:9-12	20:3-10
3. Jesus' appearances to women:				
Mary Magdalene (Jerusalem)		16:9-11		20:11-18
Other women (Jerusalem	28:9-10			
4. Guards' report to rulers (Jerusalem)	28:11-15			
5. Jesus' appearances to disciples:				
On road to Emmaus (and Simon)		16:12-13	24:13-35	
Ten disciples (Jerusalem)			24:36-43	20:19-25
Eleven disciples (Jerusalem)		16:14		20:26-31
Seven disciples by Sea of Galilee, second miracle of the fishes				21:1-25
500 disciples (I Cor. 15:5-7)	28:16-20	16:15-18		
6. The ascension (Acts 1:9-12)		16:19-20	24:44-53	

Read at least the fullest account of each event.

"HE IS NOT HERE"

At dawn on the first day of the week, an angel descended from heaven, rolled back the stone from the door of the tomb, and sat upon it; and there was a great earthquake. The angel did not roll away the stone to let Jesus out, but to show the world that He was gone. Pilate had sealed the tomb and placed a guard to watch it. When the angel came, the watchers were terrified. When the women arrived and found the tomb opened and the body of Jesus gone, they were perplexed; but there were two angels in shining apparel. One of them announced, "He is not here: for he is risen, as he said. Come, see the place where the Lord lay. And go quickly, and tell his disciples that he is risen from the dead; and, behold, he goeth before you into Galilee; there shall ye see him: lo, I have told you" (Matt. 28:6-7).

PETER AND JOHN'S VISIT TO THE TOMB

When the women told the disciples that Jesus had risen, they didn't believe them. At first the disciples thought it was just an idle tale, but Peter and John decided to see for themselves and ran for the tomb. When they saw the linen clothes that were used to wind around the body with layers of spices between, they believed. The clothes were still lying as if they were wrapped around a body; they were not thrown in wild disarray as a grave robber would have left them. The napkin that was used to cover Jesus' head was still lying in its place.

JESUS' APPEARANCES TO HIS FOLLOWERS

Jesus appeared to Mary Magdalene, to the other women, and then to two disciples walking toward Emmaus. Even though Jesus had taught very plainly about His death and resurrection, His disciples still did not understand. As He walked with the disciples, He explained to them through the

157

Scriptures that these things all had been prophesied. "Ought not Christ to have suffered these things, and to enter into his glory? And beginning at Moses and all the prophets, he expounded unto them in all the scriptures the things concerning himself" (Luke 24:26-27).

GUARDS' REPORT TO THE RULERS

Some of the guards went into the city and reported to the chief priests who assembled all the elders. They would not acknowledge that Jesus had risen from the dead. They gave the soldiers a large sum of money and told them to say, "His disciples came by night, and stole him away" (Matt. 28:13). The elders assured the soldiers that if they were reported to the governor for sleeping on guard, the elders would protect them from the governor's wrath. This explanation of the empty tomb has come down through the ages to this present day. If you will examine this explanation closely, you will see how ridiculous it is. If the soldiers were asleep, how did they know that the disciples stole Jesus' body? If they were not asleep, why did they let them steal Him?

JESUS' APPEARANCES TO HIS DISCIPLES

Jesus looked different after His resurrection. Mary Magdalene did not recognize Him at first. His disciples were frightened when He appeared in the upper room. They thought He was a spirit. He did vanish miraculously after talking with the two disciples in Emmaus, and He appeared in the upper room even though the doors were locked. It was still His body, and He showed them the prints of the nails in His hands and His feet. He told Thomas to put his hand in His side. He ate some fish and honeycomb in their presence, and He invited them to handle Him so they could witness to the fact that it was really Jesus who had risen from the grave.

SECOND MIRACULOUS DRAUGHT OF FISHES

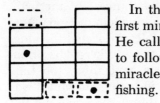 In the spring of 28, Jesus performed the first miraculous draught of fishes at the time He called Peter, Andrew, James and John to follow Him as disciples. Both times the miracles followed an unsuccessful night of fishing.

PROOFS OF RESURRECTION

Jesus showed "himself alive after his passion [suffering] by many infallible proofs, being seen of them forty days" (Acts 1:3). Jesus' appearances were not hoaxes or illusions for the following reasons:

1. He was seen repeatedly over a period of forty days.
2. He was seen by over five hundred different witnesses (I Cor. 15:6).
3. He was seen at different geographical locations both inside and outside buildings (Jerusalem, garden tomb, upper room, road to Emmaus, Mount of Olives and Galilee).
4. He was seen at different times of the day.
5. He was seen engaged in different kinds of activity (walking, eating, cooking and talking).
6. He was seen by witnesses who were most acquainted with Him.

A COMMISSION GIVEN

While in Galilee, Jesus commissioned His disciples to go to all nations and preach the gospel to every creature (Mark 16:15; Matt. 28:19-20). The kingdom had been offered to Israel and rejected. During this period of rejection, the good news is that "God so loved the world, that he gave his only begotten Son, that whosoever believeth in him should not perish, but have everlasting life" (John 3:16). The message of eternal salvation is to be proclaimed to all. Probably at this time the five hundred "brethren" mentioned in I Corinthians 15:6 saw Jesus.

In the forty days between the resurrection and the ascension, Jesus taught His disciples many things; but the main theme of His teaching concerned the kingdom of God (Acts 1:3). Just because that generation of Jews rejected the kingdom does not mean that God is not going to keep His promise. When the disciples asked Jesus concerning the time when He would restore the kingdom in Israel, He said it was not for them to know the times nor the seasons. He did not say that the kingdom would not be set up. It *will* be when He returns the second time.

In the interval between Christ's ascension and His second coming, God has a new program for His people: "that repentance and remission of sins should be preached in his name among all nations, beginning at Jerusalem. And ye are witnesses of these things" (Luke 24:47-48). This new program was to start when the Holy Spirit came. "And, behold, I send the promise of my Father upon you: but tarry ye in the city of Jerusalem, until ye be endued with power from on high" (Luke 24:49). The word translated "endued" literally means "clothed." Acts 1:8 says, "But ye shall receive power, after that the Holy Ghost is come upon you: and ye shall be witnesses unto me both in Jerusalem, and in all Judaea, and in Samaria, and unto the uttermost part of the earth."

THE ASCENSION

While Jesus was talking with His disciples on the Mount of Olives, as He blessed them, He was carried up into heaven and a cloud received Him out of their sight. While they were looking up in the sky, two men (angels) in white apparel stood by them and gave them this promise: "Ye men of Galilee, why stand ye gazing up into heaven? This same Jesus, which is taken up from you into heaven, shall so come in like manner as ye have seen him go into heaven" (Acts 1:11). "And they worshipped him [Jesus], and returned to Jerusalem with great joy: and were continually in the temple, praising and blessing God" (Luke 24:52-53).

160

And so ended the first earthly ministry of Jesus Christ the Lord. He took on human flesh and became the God-man, truly God and truly man. Through His life He revealed God's perfect standard for man. He also revealed to man what God is like. He came into the world and Himself paid the penalty for our sins, suffering in our place so that we would not have to be punished. Satan was defeated at the cross and will someday be cast in the lake of fire and brimstone. Jesus came as the Son of David, the promised Messiah and King of Israel; but His generation rejected Him. He has returned to the Father and now is manifesting His life through a new body, the church. The church is an assembly of born-again believers who have been called out from the Jews and the Gentiles. The church is the bride of Christ. The Bible promises that Christ will return to meet His church in the air and then later return as King of kings and Lord of lords to set up His kingdom on this earth to fulfill His promises to the nation of Israel. "For ye know the grace of our Lord Jesus Christ, that, though he was rich, yet for your sakes he became poor, that ye through his poverty might be rich" (II Cor. 8:9).

"O the depth of the riches both of the wisdom and knowledge of God! How unsearchable are his judgments, and his ways past finding out!" (Rom. 11:33).

QUESTIONS FOR MEDITATION

1. If you have conscientiously studied the record of the life of Christ to this point, by this time you should have answered the question Who is Jesus? Is He a liar, a lunatic, or the Lord from heaven? What is your answer? (I John 5:10-13).

2. Christ's program for His people during this age is to witness to the good news of salvation to every creature in every part of the world. You cannot go to every part of the world, but have you been faithful in the place where the Lord has put you?

161

3. The next great event in prophecy is the return of Jesus Christ for His church. If He should come today, would you be ready to meet Him?
See Appendix M.

APPENDIX A

ANGELS

The word *angel* means messenger. In the Old Testament the expression "the angel of the LORD" referred to God in angelic form (Gen. 16:1-13). In the New Testament the word *angel* (in Greek) was sometimes used for men (Luke 7:27; Rev. 1:20). In normal usage the word *angel* refers to created spiritual beings. The Bible reveals a number of facts about them:

1. They are very numerous (Matt. 26:53; Rev. 5:11).
2. They are very powerful (II Kings 19:35).
3. They sometimes are able to appear in the semblance of human form (Matt. 28:5; Mark 16:5).
4. They are ministering spirits for the heirs of salvation (Heb. 1:14). It seems as though this ministry starts with birth (Matt. 18:10) and continues through life (Ps. 34:7; 91:11). At death the angels receive or carry the departing heir into the Lord's presence (Luke 16:22).
5. Angels are to accompany Christ at His second coming (Matt. 25:31).

The Bible also contradicts some popular ideas about angels:

1. They are not glorified human beings. Believers never become angels. Matthew 22:30 says that we shall be *like* the angels. This is a figure of speech and does not say that we shall be angels. In contrast, the Bible teaches that believers will judge angels (I Cor. 6:3).
2. Angels are wise but do not have all knowledge (II Sam. 14:20; Luke 1:34).

3. All angels are not of the same class. The cherubim are mentioned in Genesis 3:24; the seraphim are mentioned in Isaiah 6:2. The word *archangel* occurs twice in Scripture (I Thess. 4:16; Jude 9). There are also evil or fallen angels (II Peter 2:4). The demons mentioned in the New Testament are usually thought to be fallen angels. Satan is a fallen angel (Isa. 14; Ezek. 28). Satan is able to appear as an angel of light (II Cor. 11:14).

MINISTRY OF ANGELS IN THE LIFE OF CHRIST

The angels began their ministry in the New Testament by announcing to Zacharias the birth of his son, John the Baptist (Luke 1:11). The angel Gabriel told Mary that she would be the mother of the Christ (Luke 1:26). An angel of the Lord appeared to Joseph in a dream and told him the child that Mary would bear was to be the Son of David, the promised Messiah (Matt. 1:20). At Jesus' birth there was a multitude of the heavenly host praising God (Luke 2:13). When Herod was determined to kill Jesus, the new king of Israel, an angel of the Lord appeared to Joseph in a dream and told him to take the young child and his mother and flee to Egypt (Matt. 2:13). After Herod died, an angel told Joseph to return from the land of Egypt (Matt. 2:19-20). The next mention of the ministry of angels occurs at the temptation of Christ. The devil tempted Jesus: "For it is written, He shall give his angels charge over thee, to keep thee: and in their hands they shall bear thee up, lest at any time thou dash thy foot against a stone" (Luke 4:10-11). After the temptation was over and the devil had left Jesus, the angels came and ministered to Him (Matt. 4:11). Jesus mentioned angels in His teaching. But they do not appear in the Bible again until near the end of His life (John 1:51; Matt. 13:39; 16:27; 18:10; Luke 15:10; Matt. 16:27; Luke 16:22; Matt. 24:36; 25:31; 25:41; 26:53).

An angel came to the garden of Gethsemane and ministered to Christ (Luke 22:43). An angel of the Lord rolled away the stone from the tomb (Matt. 28:2). The women found two angels inside the tomb (Luke 24:4; Matt. 28:5). At Jesus' ascension there were two men in white apparel (Acts 1:10). The account does not use the word *angel*, but there seems to be no doubt that they were angels.

During most of Jesus' ministry, the activities of angels were not revealed, but the fallen angels (demons) were very active. Jesus as the perfect Man had to contend with them. As God He defeated them. The Christian is involved in a spiritual warfare (Eph. 6:12-18) that can only be won through the power of God.

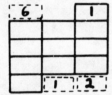

Appearances of angels

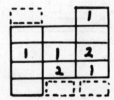

Appearance of Satan (F-26) and cases of demon possession that Jesus healed

YOUR NOTES AND REFERENCES:

APPENDIX B

BUILDINGS

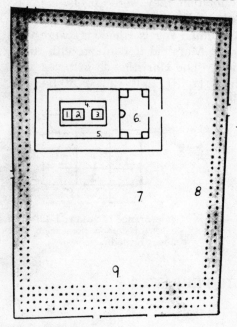

Herod's Temple — (1) holy of holies, (2) holy place, (3) altar, (4) court of the priests, (5) court of Israel, (6) court of the women, (7) court of the Gentiles, (8) Solomon's porch, (9) royal porch.

THE TEMPLE

The first temple was built by Solomon. It was destroyed in 586 B.C. by Nebuchadnezzar. Zerubbabel built the second temple and it was completed about 515 B.C. It was not as elaborate as Solomon's temple but it stood until about fifteen years before the birth of Christ. Herod the Great began the restoration of Zerubbabel's temple in 20 or 21 B.C. He did the restoration section by section, often enlarging and improving upon the former temple. It was finally completed in A.D. 64, by Herod Agrippa II, many years after Herod the Great's death. Herod's temple was destroyed by the Romans in A.D. 70.

The court of the Gentiles was about 850 feet wide and almost 1,000 feet long. It was called court of the Gentiles because this was the only part of the temple where foreigners were allowed. Women could only go as far as the court of women, which was not limited to women, however. The court of Israel was as far as the men could go. The common priests could go as far as the court of priests and into the holy place when they ministered. The high priest could go into the holy of holies only once each year on the day of atonement.

When Mary brought the Baby Jesus into the temple she probably took Him to the court of the women. It was probably in this section that Simeon and Anna saw the Baby Jesus. When Mary and Joseph came back to the temple and found Jesus talking to the doctors or rabbis He was probably on the edge of the court of the Gentiles under Solomon's porch. When Jesus cleansed the temple He drove the livestock and the money changers out of the court of the Gentiles. Jesus, who is the Lord of the temple, would never, as a man, have gone farther into the temple than the court of Israel. The details about Herod's temple are recorded by the Jewish historian Josephus who was a contemporary of Jesus.

THE SYNAGOGUE

The primary purpose of the synagogue was instruction in the Scriptures. It is not found in the Old Testament but it arose during the captivity of the intertestament period. There were many synagogues in Jerusalem; every nationality had its own (Acts 6:9). In cities outside of Jerusalem, the building was located so the congregation usually faced Jerusalem. In the interior of the synagogue the ark, or chest, was at the front, and it contained the Scriptures. The "chief seats" were near and around the ark and faced the people. These were for the elders and leading men. Jesus condemned the Pharisees because they always desired these chief seats. Gentile visitors were allowed to sit near the door, and women

167

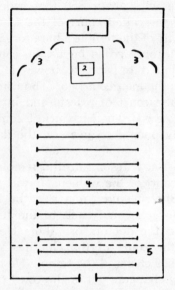

Synagogue — (1) the ark, (2) the reading desk, (3) the chief seats, (4) seats for the congregation, (5) balcony for the women.

sat in a latticed gallery (they could hear but not be seen). In front of the ark there was a platform with a reading desk, or lectern, on it. There was always a chief ruler of the synagogue and sometimes there were two other rulers. There was also a servant who was called a minister in Luke 4:20 ("attendant" in the ASV). The servant was usually the sexton, schoolmaster and constable.

Services were held on the Sabbath, on Monday and Thursday (market days), and on feast days. The program consisted of prayers, readings from the Law and the Prophets, and remarks. The readings were by an appointed order (Acts 15:21). The ruler of the synagogue might invite any suitable person he saw present to address the people (Acts 13:15). The synagogues were also used as a court of justice, and as such we read of persons being beaten and scourged in the synagogue (Matt. 10:17; 23:34; Mark 13:9; Luke 21:12). To be put out of the synagogue, or excommunicated, meant to be deprived of national privileges, and that was a punishment that was much dreaded (John 9:22; 12:42; 16:2).

168

HOUSES

Houses of common people were made of mud and bricks dried in the sun. Sometimes rough sandstones were used with mud joints between the stones. Only the rich used hewn stones. The house of the common people was usually a one-roomed building with a flat roof. There was an outside stairway to the roof, and a low wall or battlement around the edge of the roof to keep people from falling off. Especially during the hot weather, the roof was used for many purposes, and the occupants of the house often slept there at night. The windows in the houses were usually small and covered with a latticework. In good weather the cooking was usually done outside. There were no chimneys in the house, but sometimes openings were left to allow the smoke to escape.

The wealthy built houses of hewn stone and they were built around a courtyard. There was one outside door to the street. Sometimes a portion of the courtyard was covered with tile for shade. An upper room was often built on the house. This was a cool place in hot weather, and guests were often honored by giving them accommodations there. It was in an upper room that Jesus observed the Passover with His disciples; and later it was in an upper room that the disciples met after the ascension.

INN

When Mary and Joseph came to Bethlehem, "there was no room for them in the inn" (Luke 2:7). This inn was not like our modern hotel or motel. It was probably the simple Oriental khan provided by the town for travelers. It was usually a courtyard with rooms around the edge to sleep in. The lodgers would unload their beasts in the courtyard and tie them in the stalls. Sometimes the traveler would stay with his livestock if the khan was crowded. Mangers were built into the wall. The traveler would spread his own mat on the floor and provide his own food. There would not necessarily be an innkeeper in charge of the inn, but often in the larger khans there was an innkeeper who sold feed for the animals and for the travelers.

HOSPITALITY

The Israelite was noted for his hospitality to both friend and stranger. Alfred Edersheim says,

> The Rabbis enjoin this in the strongest terms. In Jerusalem no man was to account a house as only his own; and it was said, that during the pilgrim-feasts none ever wanted ready reception. . . . Of course, here also the Rabbinical order had the preference; and hospitably to entertain a sage, and to send him away with presents, was declared as meritorious as to have offered the daily sacrifices. . . . The very manner in which a host is to bear himself towards his guests is prescribed. He is to look pleased when entertaining his guests, to wait upon them himself, to promise little and to give much, etc. At the same time it was also caustically added: "Consider all men as if they were robbers, but treat them as if each were Rabbi Gamaliel himself!"*

Upon entering, a guest would exchange bows with the host, say a greeting or a blessing on the house and receive a kiss (Luke 7:45). He would remove his shoes or sandals and be offered water to wash his feet. A servant would assist in the foot washing; Jesus did this for His disciples (John 13:4-5). David speaks of the Lord anointing his head with oil (Ps. 23:5); head anointing was a custom in New Testament times also (Luke 7:46). Sharing a meal was considered a special act of hospitality.

It was considered a terrible offense to abuse hospitality or to do evil to anyone who had been your host. The host by accepting a guest felt responsible to protect him. Perhaps this is why David rejoiced in the protection of God when he

*Alfred Edersheim, *Sketches of Jewish Social Life* (Grand Rapids: Wm. B. Eerdmans Publishing Co., 1950), pp. 47-49.

said, "Thou preparest a table before me in the presence of mine enemies" (Ps. 23:5).

YOUR NOTES AND REFERENCES:

APPENDIX C

CHRONOLOGICAL BIBLE-MARKING

One of the most important parts of this study course is the marking of your Bible so that you can know the chronological order of the events in the Gospels. Basically the gospel events are given in chronological order. They may skip several months or, as Matthew, skip a whole year (A.D. 27). But for all practical purposes they are in order. The one big exception is Matthew 8–12. This section is grouped according to themes. If you will write F-26, Sp-27, or S-27, for instance (season, year) in the margin of your Bible at the proper verse, you will be able to locate any event in the Gospels within about a four-month period. This will require only from nine to eleven marks in each gospel.

This is your guide for marking the gospel of Mark:

VERSE	SYMBOL
Mark 1:9	F-26
1:14	F-27
1:16	SP-28
2:23	S-28
4:1	F-28
6:1	SP-29
6:30	S-29
10:1	SP-30
11:1	F.W.
16:1	P.R.

171

ST. MARK

CHAPTER 1

THE beginning of the gospel of Jesus Christ, the Son of God;

2 As it is written in the prophets, Behold, I send my messenger before thy face, which shall prepare thy way before thee.

3 The voice of one crying in the wilderness, Prepare ye the way of the Lord, make his paths straight.

4 John did baptize in the wilderness, and preach the baptism of repentance for the remission of sins.

5 And there went out unto him all the land of Judea, and they of Jerusalem, and were all baptized of him in the river of Jordan, confessing their sins.

6 And John was clothed with camel's hair, and with a girdle of a skin about his loins; and he did eat locusts and wild honey;

7 And preached, saying, There cometh one mightier than I after me, the latchet of whose shoes I am not worthy to stoop down and unloose.

8 I indeed have baptized you with water: but he shall baptize you with the Holy Ghost.

9 And it came to pass in those days, that Jesus came from Nazareth of Galilee, and was baptized of John in Jordan.

10 And straightway coming up out of the water, he saw the heavens opened, and the Spirit like a dove descending upon him:

11 And there came a voice from heaven, *saying*, Thou art my beloved Son, in whom I am well pleased.

12 And immediately the Spirit driveth him into the wilderness.

13 And he was there in the wilderness forty days tempted of Satan; and was with the wild beasts; and the angels ministered unto him.

14 Now after that John was put in prison, Jesus came into Galilee, preaching the gospel of the kingdom of God,

15 And saying, The time is fulfilled, and the kingdom of God is at hand: repent ye, and believe the gospel.

16 Now as he walked by the sea of Galilee, he saw Simon and Andrew his brother casting a net into the sea: for they were fishers.

17 And Jesus said unto them, Come ye after me, and I will make you to become fishers of men.

18 And straightway they forsook their nets, and followed him.

19 And when he had gone a little further thence, he saw James the *son of* Zĕb'ē-dēe, and John his brother, who also were in the ship mending their nets.

20 And straightway he called them: and they left their father Zĕb'ē-dēe in the ship with the hired servants, and went after him.

21 And they went into Cȧ-pĕr'nā-ŭm; and straightway on the sabbath day he entered into the synagogue, and taught.

22 And they were astonished at his doctrine: for he taught them as one that had authority, and not as the scribes.

23 And there was in their synagogue a man with an unclean spirit; and he cried out,

24 Saying, Let *us* alone; what have we to do with thee, thou Jesus of Nazareth? art thou come to destroy us? I know thee who thou art, the Holy One of God.

25 And Jesus rebuked him, saying, Hold thy peace, and come out of him.

26 And when the unclean spirit had torn him, and cried with a loud voice, he came out of him.

27 And they were all amazed, insomuch that they questioned among themselves, saying, What thing is this? what new doctrine *is* this? for with authority commandeth he even the unclean spirits, and they do obey him.

28 And immediately his fame spread abroad throughout all the region round about Galilee.

29 And forthwith, when they were come out of the synagogue, they entered into the house of Simon and Andrew, with James and John.

30 But Simon's wife's mother lay sick of a fever; and anon they tell him of her.

31 And he came and took her by the hand, and lifted her up; and immediately the fever left her, and she ministered unto them.

By placing these ten marks you can divide the gospel of Mark chronologically. Following the chart here given, mark the other three gospels in the same way.

How to Mark the Gospels Chronologically for the Earthly Ministry of Christ

Date	Matthew	Mark	Luke	John	Abbre-viation
Fall 26	3:13	1:9	3:21	1:19	F-26
Spring 27				2:1	Sp-27
Summer 27	4:12			2:13	S-27
Fall 27		1:14	4:14	4:1	F-27
Spring 28	4:13	1:16	4:16		Sp-28
Summer 28	5:1 (Matthew 8—12 is not in order.)	2:23	6:1	5:1	S-28
Fall 28	13:1	4:1	8:4		F-28
Spring 29	13:54	6:1	9:1		Sp-29
Summer 29	14:13	6:30	9:10	6:1	S-29
Fall 29			10:1	7:11	F-29
Spring 30	19:1	10:1	13:22	10:40	Sp-30
Final Week	21:1	11:1	19:29	11:55	F.W.
Post-Resur-rection	28:1-20	16:1-20	24:1-53	20:1—21:25	P.R.

FINDING THE DATE OF AN EVENT

Suppose you are studying the transfiguration account in Luke 9:27-36 and you want to know when it happened. All you have to do is to start looking backward in your margin until you come to the first date sign. In this case it would be at Luke 9:10, and beside it would be S-29. Always go backward to the date sign. Suppose your pastor is preaching on the feeding of the five thousand in John 6:10-13. If you go back in your Bible to the first date sign, you will find it at John 6:1, and the date will be S-29. Suppose you are reading the account of the demons being cast out of the man and into the swine in Mark 5:13. If you look back in the margin, you will find the date sign F-28 beside Mark 4:1.

APPENDIX D

DEATH, FUNERALS, AND BURIAL CUSTOMS

As a whole the Jews believed in a life after death. (The Sadducees did not.) The Talmud taught that paradise and hell were both created before the earth. They looked upon an early death as a judgment from God.

The Israelites were a very emotional people. In times of sorrow and death they would wail and cry. Sometimes they would wear sackcloth and put ashes on their heads. On the death of a member of the family they would rend their garments. This was usually done in a prescribed way: the tunic was torn about the width of a hand at the neck.

PREPARATION FOR BURIAL

Very soon after death, the body was washed and wrapped in linen cloth. Sometimes sweet-smelling spices were wrapped in the folds of the cloth. Each member of the body (each arm and leg) was wrapped separately, and a napkin was wound about the head. The Jews did not practice embalming nor cremation.*

FUNERAL PROCESSION

Burying places were outside the cities. The body was ordinarily taken to its final resting place on an exposed bier. According to Alfred Edersheim, the order of mourners was different in Galilee than it was in Judaea. In Galilee, first

*Edwin Cone Bissell, *Biblical Antiquities* (Philadelphia: American Sunday-School Union, 1888), p. 58.

came the women; second, the bier with its bearers; third, the hired mourners; fourth, special friends; and last, the general company. In Judaea the hired mourners went before the bier. The women went first because "woman, who brought death into our world, ought to lead the way in the funeral procession," a Jewish commentary explains.†

If a person met a funeral procession it was considered impolite if he did not join the general company and go at least a short distance with it (Luke 7:12). (The exception was a wedding procession, which had the right of way over a funeral procession.) The bearers often changed, and at these stops short addresses were sometimes delivered. At the grave there sometimes was a funeral oration.

PLACES OF BURIAL

If the grave was in a public cemetery, at least a foot and a half must separate each grave. The rabbis said that sepulchers or caves ought to be at least six cubits square. The door might be rectangular, built of stone and fitted with a hinge, but the more common method was to use a cylindrical stone that rolled in a groove in front of the opening. The women were concerned about the stone at the Lord's tomb because it was "very great" (Mark 16:3-5). The poor people often used natural caves (Luke 8:27).

†Edersheim, *Sketches of Jewish Social Life* (Grand Rapids: Wm. B. Eerdmans Publishing Co., 1950), p. 170.

MOURNERS

It was customary, if a family could afford it, to hire professional mourners to join in the lamentations. These were generally women. The mourning had already started when the Lord arrived at Jairus' house (Mark 5:36-40). The mourning started at the moment of death and continued until after the funeral which usually took place on the same day.

DEPARTURE OF THE SOUL

The rabbinical teaching was that the soul wandered around the grave for three days seeking an opportunity to return to the body. By the fourth day decomposition of the body was such that the soul left the body to itself. Friends often visited the tomb during this time, probably with the idea that they would be closer to the soul of their loved one. Lazarus had been dead four days—beyond any hope according to the common idea.‡

Jesus restored three people to life: the widow's son, Jarius' daughter, and His friend Lazarus. He also healed the demon-possessed men who were living in a graveyard (Luke 8:27). He Himself was buried in the garden tomb with a stone rolled in front of the door.

YOUR NOTES AND REFERENCES:

‡James M. Freeman, *Hand-book of Bible Manners and Customs* (New York: Hunt & Eaton, 1889), p. 431.

176

APPENDIX E

EATING HABITS AND CUSTOMS

HAND-WASHING

Ceremonial hand-washing was a big item of contention between the scribes and Jesus. The Talmud says, "It is better to go four miles to water than to incur guilt by neglecting hand-washing." One rabbi said, "He who eats bread without hand-washing is as if he went in to a harlot." Another said, "Three sins bring poverty after them, and to slight hand-washing is one."

Ceremonial hand-washing should not be confused with normal cleanliness and hand hygiene. Cunningham Geikie describes the ritual in the following words:

> It was laid down that the hands were first to be washed clean. The tips of the ten fingers were then joined and lifted up so that the water ran down to the elbows, then turned down so that it might run off to the ground. Fresh water was poured on them as they were lifted up, and twice again as they hung down. The washing itself was to be done by rubbing the fist of one hand in the hollow of the other. When the hands were washed before eating they must be held upwards; when after it, downwards, but so that the water should not run beyond the knuckles. The vessel used must be held first in the right, then in the left hand; the water was to be poured first on the right, then on the left hand, and at every third time the words repeated "Blessed art Thou who hast given us the command to wash the hands." It was keenly disputed whether the cup of blessing or the hand-washing should come first; whether the towel used should be laid on the table or on the couch; and whether the table was to be cleared before the final washing or after it.*

*Cunningham Geikie, *Life and Words of Christ* (New York: D. Appleton & Co., 1880), II, 203-4.

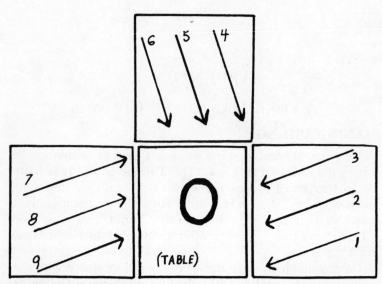

EATING HABITS

The Jews did not use knives, forks and spoons to eat their meals. Meat was usually served from a large single dish and eaten with the fingers. Sometimes bread was used as a means of conveying food to the mouth.

In Old Testament times the Jews would sit cross-legged on the floor and eat from a low table. In New Testament times most people reclined while eating. The word for recline is the word that is used at the feeding of both the four thousand and five thousand. This custom came from the Romans. They used a triclinium. It had couches on three sides. Originally the couches were each large enough to hold three persons, but the Jews were often said to have couches that held more than that number.†

The couches were provided with a cushion for the left elbow on which the guest rested while he used his right hand to eat with. The diners lay on a diagonal on the couches. The fourth side of the table was left open so that the servant

†Edwin Cone Bissell, *Biblical Antiquities* (Philadelphia: American Sunday-School Union, 1888), p. 83.

could bring food to the table. There were two different kinds of tables used, a narrow table that went along the front edge of each couch or a larger table that sat in the center.‡ This custom of reclining explains how John at the last Passover was leaning on Jesus' bosom and talking to Him, and how any of the disciples could have dipped in the dish with Jesus.

In the diagram, the section on the right was the place of honor with the first place on each couch the most highly esteemed. Luke 14:7-11 speaks of "chief rooms," "highest room" and "lowest room." Room would be more accurately translated "place." The last position on the left would be the lowest "room."

People who were not guests were often allowed to enter as spectators. This custom explains how the "woman who was a sinner" entered and later anointed Jesus' feet (first anointing, S-28).

YOUR NOTES AND REFERENCES:

APPENDIX F

FEASTS OF ISRAEL

In this book the feasts are one of the key methods of dating and dividing up the Lord's ministry into time periods. The

‡*International Standard Bible Encyclopaedia* (Grand Rapids: Wm. B. Eerdmans Publishing Co., 1943), III, 2015.

feasts were an important part of normal Jewish lite. They not only had great spiritual significance but were also social occasions. In type they point toward the ministry of Christ. Leviticus 23 gives an account of the seven great feasts of the Lord.

PASSOVER FEAST

The Passover Feast was a memorial of the redemption and deliverance of the children of Israel from Egypt. The Passover lamb was selected four days before the Passover which was celebrated on the fourteenth day of Nisan (Exodus 12:2). Christ our "passover" was sacrificed for us (I Cor. 5:7).

FEAST OF UNLEAVENED BREAD

Israel was to put away all leaven from their homes. This feast began on the day after the Passover and continued for seven days (Lev. 23:6-8). Here leaven represents sin. The unleavened bread is typical of Christ in His holiness working out our redemption, giving strength for the journey of life and for the "walk" of fellowship with Him (I Cor. 5:7-8).

FEAST OF FIRSTFRUITS

The second day after the Passover, the Feast of the Firstfruits was to be celebrated. After the children of Israel settled in the land of Canaan they were to go into the fields, take some of the first stalks of ripened grain, and wave this sheaf as an offering to the Lord as an expression of thanksgiving.

This feast foreshadowed the resurrection of Christ. He as a "corn of wheat" (John 12:24) died on the Passover, but He arose at the Feast of Firstfruits, being the firstfruits of the resurrection (I Cor. 15:22-23).

FEAST OF PENTECOST

This feast came fifty days after the Feast of Firstfruits at the end of the grain harvest. The word *pentecost* means fifty.

Fifty days after Christ arose from the grave the church was born. He had ascended to heaven ten days previously. It was at this time that the "new body" of Christ was formed and He began to call out a people for His name from both Jews and Gentiles. Between the Feast of Pentecost and the next feast is an interval of about four months. This interval represents the present age.

FEAST OF TRUMPETS

The Feast of Trumpets was observed on the first day of Tishri, the seventh month, and began a new series of feasts. During the wilderness wanderings two silver trumpets were made from the atonement money. They were used to call the assembly, and to signal the journeyings, the day of Atonement, the year of Jubilee, the anointing of kings and the dedication of Solomon's temple. The trumpets were sounded at this feast. Typically they represent the regathering of the children of Israel from among the nations of the world.

FEAST OF ATONEMENT

This day of expiation was on the tenth day of the same month, Tishri. It was for fasting, repentance and confession of sin. It was upon this day that the high priest went into the holy of holies and sprinkled blood before and upon the mercy seat. This typified the covering (atonement) of Israel's sins and was a promise of Christ's work on the cross as the Lamb of God. This feast is not mentioned in the New Testament.

FEAST OF TABERNACLES

This feast began on the fifteenth day of the month Tishri and lasted for seven days. During this feast the people lived in booths made of branches. It commemorated the forty years of wandering in the wilderness.

All male Jews were to go to Jerusalem for the three main feasts: Passover, Pentecost and Tabernacles. During the Feast of Tabernacles Jerusalem would be covered with little booths: on the housetops and in courtyards and fields. Typically this feast looks forward to the time when Israel no more will be wandering through the wilderness of the world but will be in their promised kingdom.

FEAST OF PURIM

This feast, celebrated one month before the Passover, commemorated the deliverance of the Jews in the time of Esther (Esther 9:26). It is not mentioned in the New Testament.

FEAST OF DEDICATION

This feast was celebrated on the twenty-fifth day of the Jewish month of Chislev (Nov.-Dec.). In the inter-testament period Antiochus Epiphanes plundered Jerusalem and offered a sow upon the altar of the temple. In 165 B.C. Judas Maccabaeus recaptured the city of Jerusalem and rededicated the temple. The feast lasted for eight days. This feast is mentioned once in John 10:22.

YOUR NOTES AND REFERENCES:

APPENDIX G

GEOGRAPHY

FOUR NATURAL DIVISIONS

Palestine has four natural divisions:
1. Seacoast plain
2. Mountain range
3. Jordan Valley
4. Eastern tableland

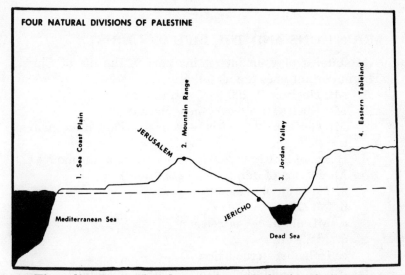

FOUR NATURAL DIVISIONS OF PALESTINE

1. Sea Coast Plain
JERUSALEM
2. Mountain Range
3. Jordan Valley
4. Eastern Tableland
Mediterranean Sea
JERICHO
Dead Sea

The adjacent sectional map shows Palestine from east to west on a line even with Jerusalem. Notice that Jerusalem is 2,600 feet above sea level. The north end of the shore of the Dead Sea (south end of the Jordan Valley) is 1,300 feet below sea level, and the sea is 1,300 feet deep or 2,600 feet below sea level.

FIVE BODIES OF WATER IN PALESTINE

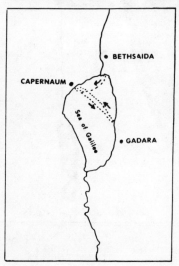

BETHSAIDA
CAPERNAUM
Sea of Galilee
GADARA

1. Mediterranean Sea (or Great Sea)
2. Lake Merom (2×3 miles, 9-16 feet deep)
3. Sea of Galilee (7×14 miles, 130-150 feet deep)
4. Dead Sea (9½×48 miles, north end 1,300 feet deep, south end 8-14 feet deep)
5. Jordan River (source to Lake Merom, 26 miles; Lake Merom to Sea of Galilee, 13 miles; Sea of Galilee to Dead Sea, 65 miles; total length, 200 miles)

183

MOUNTAINS AND THE LIFE OF CHRIST

Mountains play an interesting part in the life of Christ. The important ones are as follows:

1. Mt. Hermon (9,200 feet)—transfiguration
2. Mt. Ebal (3,075 feet)—near Sychar
3. Mt. Gerizim (2,850 feet)—conversation with woman at the well
4. Horns of Hattin (1,200 feet)—sermon on the mount (?)
5. Mountains of Jerusalem (2,600 feet)
    a. Mt. Moriah—temple
    b. Mt. Zion
    c. Mt. of Olives—ascension
    d. Mt. Acra
    e. Golgotha—crucifixion
6. Mt. of Temptation (exact location unknown)

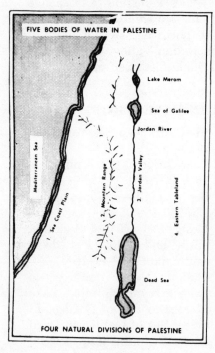

FOUR NATURAL DIVISIONS OF PALESTINE

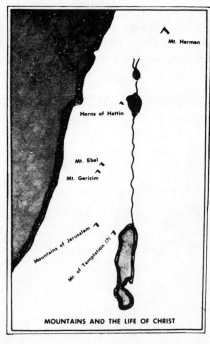

MOUNTAINS AND THE LIFE OF CHRIST

TEN COUNTRIES OR REGIONS CONNECTED WITH THE LIFE OF CHRIST

1. Galilee
2. Samaria
3. Judaea
4. Peraea
5. Ituraea
6. Egypt
7. Decapolis (ten free cities north of Peraea)
8. Syria
9. Idumaea
10. Phoenicia (about Tyre and Sidon)

TEN COUNTRIES OR REGIONS IN THE LIFE OF CHRIST

ROADS

185

ROADS

The most important road in the land of Palestine was the one that went from Damascus (1), to Capernaum (2), to Joppa (4), to Gaza (5), and then on to Egypt. This was the trade route as well as the traditional route of invasion. The other cities numbered on the map are Bethlehem (6), Jerusalem (7), Bethany (8), Jericho (9) and Nazareth (3).

YOUR NOTES AND REFERENCES:

FIFTEEN CITIES IN THE LIFE OF CHRIST

There are fifteen cities that are mentioned as being visited by Christ. They are listed with the events and time period:

CAPERNAUM

1. Nobleman's son healed (Jesus was in Cana), F-27
2. Demoniac healed on Sabbath, SP-28
3. Peter's mother-in-law healed, SP-28
4. Man let through roof delivered, SP-28
5. Call of Matthew and his feast, SP-28
6. Man with a withered hand restored, S-28
7. Centurion's servant healed, S-28
8. First anointing of Jesus' feet, S-28
9. Demon-possessed, blind, dumb man healed and Jesus accused of working by power of devil, S-28
10. Family and friends think Jesus is crazy, attempt to take Him home, S-28
11. Jairus' daughter raised, F-28

12. Woman who touched Christ's garment healed, F-28
13. Two blind men, F-28
14. Dumb demoniac, F-28
15. Bread of life discourse, S-29
16. Coin in fish's mouth, S-29

JERUSALEM

1. First Passover, S-27
2. Cleansing of temple, S-27
3. Nicodemus' interview, S-27
4. Man at the pool, S-28
5. Feast of Tabernacles, F-29
6. Man born blind healed, F-29
7. Feast of Dedication, F-29
8. Final week and some post-resurrection appearances, SP-30

CANA

1. First miracle—water into wine, SP-27
2. Nobleman's son healed in Capernaum from Cana, F-27 (second miracle in Cana)

BETHABARA

1. Baptism of Jesus, F-26
2. Location of Jesus when Lazarus died, SP-30 (Bethany beyond the Jordan)

SYCHAR

1. Woman at the well, F-27

MACHAERUS

1. John the Baptist imprisoned, S-27
2. John the Baptist killed, SP-29

JERICHO

1. Two blind men healed, SP-30
2. Zacchaeus, SP-30

BETHANY
1. Home of Mary, Martha, Lazarus—supper, F-29
2. Lazarus raised, SP-30
3. Second anointing of Jesus' feet, SP-30

BETHSAIDA
1. Blind man healed, S-29
2. 5,000 fed near here, S-29

DECAPOLIS
1. Feeding of 4,000, S-29
2. Deaf and dumb man healed, S-29
3. Demoniacs in graveyard delivered, F-28 (Gadara)

NAIN
1. Widow's son raised, S-28

BETHLEHEM
1. Jesus' birth, 5 or 6 B.C.

NAZARETH
1. Jesus at home, 4 B.C. to A.D. 27
2. First rejection, SP-28
3. Second rejection, SP-29

EPHRAIM
1. Avoiding the Jews, SP-30

EMMAUS
1. With two disciples after resurrection, SP-30

CITIES IN THE LIFE OF CHRIST

JERUSALEM

Jerusalem was the site of many important buildings and events: temple (1), Tower of Antonia, Roman garrison where Pilate stayed while in Jerusalem (2), traditional location of the last supper (3), traditional location of Caiaphas' house (4), Herod's palace (5), hall or temple where Sanhedrin met (6), Calvary (7), and Gethsemane (8). There are four important events connected with the Mount of Olives: Olivet discourse, arrest, ascension, and Christ's promised second coming.

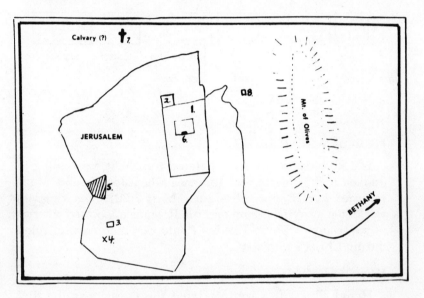

APPENDIX H

THE HEROD FAMILY

HEROD THE GREAT

Herod the Great ruled Palestine from 37 to 4 B.C. He captured Jerusalem in 37 B.C. and was crowned king by Augustus Caesar through Mark Antony's influence. He started rebuilding the temple in 20 B.C. He was a harsh and bloodthirsty old man who murdered his favorite wife and three of his sons. It was completely in character for him to order the murder of the Bethlehem babies.

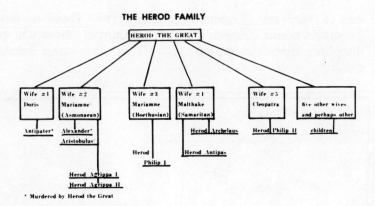

THE HEROD FAMILY

* Murdered by Herod the Great

HEROD ARCHELAUS

Herod Archelaus, a son of Herod the Great, was ruling in Judaea and Samaria and Idumaea when Joseph and Mary returned from Egypt with Jesus (Matt 2:22). His kingdom was taken away from him and the Romans appointed a series of governors of which Pontius Pilate was the one who ruled during Christ's ministry.

HEROD PHILIP I

Herod Philip I, a son of Herod the Great, was the first husband of Herodias and the father of Salome. He never ruled.

HEROD PHILIP II

Herod Philip II, a son of Herod the Great, ruled from 4 B.C. until A.D. 34. He was the Tetrarch of Ituraea. He was the best ruler among the Herod family and, relatively speaking, was fair and just. He married Salome, the dancer, his brother's daughter.

HEROD ANTIPAS

Herod Antipas, a son of Herod the Great and a brother of Archelaus, ruled as the Tetrarch of Galilee and Peraea from 4 B.C. to A.D. 39. He was mean and crafty. Jesus once called

190

him a fox. He and Pilate were enemies until after the trial of Jesus.

HERODIAS

Herodias was the daughter of Aristobulus, granddaughter of Herod the Great, and sister of Herod Agrippa I. She was first married to Herod Philip I and left him to live with Herod Antipas.

SALOME

Salome was the daughter of Herodias and Herod Philip I. At the banquet that Herod Antipas gave she danced before him. It was to her that he promised he would give up to half of his kingdom. Her mother, Herodias, persuaded her to ask for the head of John the Baptist. She later married Herod Philip II.

HEROD AGRIPPA I

Herod Agrippa I ruled from A.D. 37 to 44. He was the brother of Herodias and a grandson of Herod the Great. He is the one in the book of Acts that beheaded the Apostle James and imprisoned Peter.

HEROD AGRIPPA II

Herod Agrippa II, a great-grandson of Herod the Great, ruled from A.D. 52 to 70. He was king of part of Judaea, and Bernice and Drusilla were his sisters. Paul made his defense before him.

MEMORY HELPS

The kingdom of Herod Philip II is shaped like a teacup with the handle broken off. As a memory help, think of the fact that you "fill up" a teacup. This will help you remember the ruler (Philip). The handle looks like it is broken off— there is something missing. Philip lost something—he lost his heart to Salome, the dancer.

191

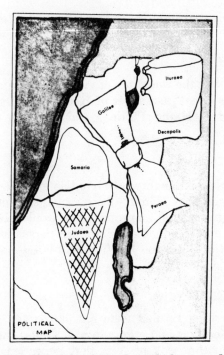

POLITICAL MAP

The kingdom ruled by Herod Archelaus and later Pilate is shaped like an ice cream cone. An ice cream cone has two distinct parts, the ice cream and the cone. Even though this kingdom was one politically, it was in two distinct parts, Judaea and Samaria. They didn't mix and hated each other. The very top corner of Samaria on the seacoast includes Mount Carmel where Elijah met the prophets of Baal. To help remember this, just think of a "caramel" topping on the ice cream cone.

The kingdom ruled by Herod Antipas is shaped like a bow tie with half of it on each side of the Jordan River: Galilee and Peraea (see the map). Sometimes while a person is eating, his tie will become spotted. There are three spots on this kingdom: Lake Merom, the Sea of Galilee and the Dead Sea. There are three spots on the record of Herod Antipas: (1) He stole Herod Philip I's wife Herodias. (2) He

192

beheaded John the Baptist. (3) Jesus was sent before him by Pilate for trial.

YOUR NOTES AND REFERENCES:

APPENDIX I

INTERTESTAMENT PERIOD

When the New Testament opened, the scene was very different from the one seen as the Old Testament closed, when Persia was ruling over Palestine. Five countries had ruled over Palestine:

1. Persia, 538-333 B.C.
2. Greece, 333-323 B.C. (under Alexander the Great)
3. Egypt, 323-204 B.C.
4. Syria, 204-167 B.C. (When Antiochus Epiphanes plundered Jerusalem, offered a sow on the altar of the temple, and tried to enforce the Hellenization of Jews, the Maccabaean rebellion broke out. Although there was much fighting, the Jews were practically independent from 167-63 B.C.)
5. Rome, from 63 B.C. onward

FIVE NEW PARTIES

In the New Testament times five new parties were active that were not seen in the Old Testament. The first three listed were religious and the last two were political:

193

1. Pharisees (see Appendix R)
2. Sadducees (see Appendix R)
3. Essenes (see Appendix R)
4. Herodians (see Appendix Z)
5. Zealots (see Appendix Z)

FIVE NEW INSTITUTIONS

Five new institutions appeared upon the New Testament scene without explanation:
1. Synagogue (see Appendix B)
2. Sanhedrin (see Appendix S)
3. Publicans (see Appendix V)
4. Scribes (see Appendix V)
5. Oral law (see Appendix L)

FIVE FAVORABLE FACTORS FOR THE PROCLAMATION OF THE GOSPEL

1. The iron rule of Rome kept the world in a state of peace without any major wars.
2. Greek was then the universal language, the language of culture. Later the New Testament was written in Greek.
3. The Jewish dispersion, to some extent, caused knowledge of the true God to spread through all parts of the known world. The Septuagint (Greek translation of the Old Testament) made the Word of God available in a language most could understand.
4. Roman roads made it possible to travel with some degree of speed and safety.
5. There was worldwide skepticism concerning pagan gods. The great philosophies of the world had given their answers to the purpose or mystery of life and had been found wanting.

YOUR NOTES AND REFERENCES:

APPENDIX J

JEWISH PRIESTS

HIGH PRIESTS

When the children of Israel were in the wilderness, God instituted the priesthood. The priest spoke to God for sinful man and offered sacrifices for reconciliation. Aaron was made the first high priest (Lev. 8:1—10:20). The position was to be for a lifetime. There could be only one high priest at a time and he must be of the family of Aaron and in the tribe of Levi. The oldest son normally inherited this position.

He was not to have physical blemishes. This in type points to our great High Priest, Jesus Christ, who is holy and unblemished by sin. Christ was not an earthly priest because He was of the tribe of Judah. Hebrews 5:1—7:28 points out the superiority of the priesthood of Christ, it being an unending priesthood "after the order of Melchisedec" (7:17).

During the ministry of Christ the high priesthood had degenerated into a political position. The Jewish historian Josephus says that there were twenty-eight different high priests from the accession of Herod until the destruction of Jerusalem in A.D. 70. Some of the more important ones were Annas, Eleazar (son of Annas), Joseph Caiaphas, son-in-law of Annas and high priest during Christ's ministry), Jonathan (son of Annas) and Theophilus (son of Annas) from whom Paul received letters to go to Damascus (Acts 9:1, 14).

CHIEF PRIESTS

The priesthood was divided into twenty-four courses, or groups. There was a chief priest over each group of priests. Each group in turn ministered in the temple for one week. There is some evidence that the term "chief priests" was also used of deposed former high priests.

195

COMMON PRIESTS

The common priests went up to Jerusalem when it was their time to minister. Zacharias, John the Baptist's father, was a priest of the course of Abia. It was while he was ministering in the temple that an angel of the Lord appeared to him and told him he was going to have a son (Luke 1:5, 8-13).

YOUR NOTES AND REFERENCES:

APPENDIX K
Kings, Procurators, Emperors

In the year 63 B.C. Palestine came under the rule of Rome. Rome at this time was a republic, but in 31 B.C. the imperial forces defeated the army and navy of the republic, and Augustus became the first emperor. He ruled until A.D. 14 (Luke 2:1). He allowed himself to be deified and worshiped as god.

Tiberius was the second emperor and ruled from A.D. 14 to 37. He was the Caesar that was ruling during Jesus' ministry and death. Pilate is said to have sent him a report of Jesus' death.

KINGS

The family of kings in New Testament times is the Herod family. Herod the Great was born in 74 B.C. in Idumaea, the territory south of Judaea. He was made king in 37 B.C. Mark Antony helped him get his throne, but after Antony's defeat by Augustus, Herod won Augustus' favor and retained his throne. His kingdom included: Idumaea, Judaea, Samaria, Galilee, Peraea, and Ituraea. After his death the kingdom was divided. See Appendix H.

PROCURATORS

After Herod the Great died, his son Archelaus ruled Judaea, Idumaea and Samaria until A.D. 6 when he was deposed. This territory was then governed by Roman procurators until A.D. 42. Pontius Pilate is the fifth procurator. He began his rule in A.D. 26, the same year the Lord began His ministry. Pilate was born in Spain and was a ruthless character. He was under investigation by the Roman senate at the time of Christ's trial. In 36 he was banished to Gaul.

APPENDIX L

THE LAW, WRITTEN AND ORAL, AND THE SABBATH

The word *law* is used several ways: sometimes of the Ten Commandments, at other times of the Old Testament as a whole; it also referred to the first five books of the Bible, written by Moses.

TARGUMS

The Targums are paraphrases of the Old Testament into Aramaic. This became the common language after the exile in Babylon. A scribe would read the Hebrew scripture and then give the translation and meaning in Aramaic. The Targums were not written until the Christian era, but were passed down orally.

ORAL LAW

As the scribes and rabbis studied the Scriptures, they accumulated a vast collection of interpretations, amplifications and additional regulations. At the time of Christ they were considered just as binding, if not more so, than the written law itself.

TALMUD

In the second century A.D. the oral law was committed to writing. It is one part of the Talmud, the Mishna. The other part of the Talmud is the Gemara, commentaries upon the Mishna.

The Lord came into direct conflict with the oral law and consequently against the scholarly opinions and public sentiment of the day. In the Sermon on the Mount He used the expression "Ye have heard that it was said by them of old time . . ." (Matt. 5:21, 27, 31, 33, 38, 43) when He referred to the oral law. Then as He taught with authority, He said, "But I say unto you. . ." (Matt. 5:22). This does not mean that all the oral law was bad—there were many good things in it. When Jesus quoted Scripture He would usually use the expression "It is written . . ." (Matt. 4:4). In the Sermon on the Mount He contrasted the best of the sayings of the oral law with God's standard of righteousness: "For I say unto you, That except your righteousness shall exceed the righteousness of the scribes and Pharisees, ye shall in no case enter into the kingdom of heaven" (Matt. 5:20).

The seriousness of the situation is described by Jesus: "Full well ye reject the commandment of God, that ye may keep your own tradition. . . . Making the word of God of none effect through your tradition, which ye have delivered: and many such things do ye" (Mark 7:9-13).

SABBATH

One of the big controversies between the scribes and Pharisees and Jesus was on how to keep the sabbath.

God, having completed the work of creation in six days, blessed the seventh day and hallowed it. The first use of the name sabbath occurs in Exodus 16:23. It is used of not only the seventh day (Exodus 16:26) but (1) a year (Lev. 25:2, 4, 8); (2) the first day of the Feast of Trumpets (Lev. 23:24); (3) the day of Atonement (Lev. 16:31); and (4) the first day of the Feast of Unleavened Bread (Lev. 23:11). It lasted from evening to evening (Lev. 23:32).

Two whole sections of the Mishna are occupied with the regulations for observing the sabbath. When the Lord healed the sick on the sabbath it made the Jews very angry. When His disciples plucked grain and ate it, the scribes considered that they broke the sabbath in two ways: plucking the grain was reaping, and rubbing it was threshing. The Lord's reply was "The sabbath was made for man, and not man for the sabbath: therefore the Son of man is Lord also of the sabbath" (Mark 2:27-28).

YOUR NOTES AND REFERENCES:

APPENDIX M

MIRACLES

The miracles of Jesus can be divided into four main classes:

1. Miracles over nature
2. Miracles of physical healing

3. Miracles over demons

4. Miracles over death

Only a few of Jesus' miracles are recorded. General groups of miracles are mentioned (Matt. 4:23-24; 9:35; Mark 6:56; Luke 4:40-41; 5:15; 6:17-19; 7:21-23; John 2:23; 3:2; 4:45; 20:30; 21:25). John records eight specifically as signs "that ye might believe that Jesus is the Christ, the Son of God; and that believing ye might have life through his name" (John 20:31).

```
┌ ─ ─ ┐ ┌───┐
└ ─ ─ ┘ │   │
┌───┬───┬───┐
│ 1 │ X │ 1 │
├───┼───┼───┤
│ 5 │ 5 │ 6 │
├───┼───┼───┤
│ X │ 8 │ 3 │
├───┼─ ─┼─ ─┤
│ 4 │ 2 │ 1 │
└───┴ ─ ┴ ─ ┘
```

Some of the groups of miracles occurred in S-27 and Sp-29 so that beginning with Sp-27 with the changing of water to wine and continuing on until Christ's ascension there are miracles in every period, most of them in S-29.

YOUR NOTES AND REFERENCES:

TIME CHART OF MIRACLES IN THE MINISTRY OF CHRIST
AND THE CHAPTERS IN WHICH THEY ARE FOUND

	Matthew	Mark	Luke	John
SP-27 1. Water into wine				2
F-27 2. Nobleman's son healed				4

	Matthew	Mark	Luke	John
SP-28				
3. First draught of fishes			5	
4. Demoniac healed on Sabbath		1	4	
5. Peter's mother-in-law cured	8	1	4	
6. Leper healed	8	1	5	
7. Roof opened for sick man	9	2	5	
S-28				
8. Man at the pool				5
9. Man with withered hand	12	3	6	
10. Centurion's servant healed	8		7	
11. Widow's son raised			7	
12. Demon-possessed, blind, dumb man	12	3		
F-28				
13. Stilling the tempest on the sea	8	4	8	
14. Demoniacs in graveyard	8	5	8	
15. Jairus' daughter raised	9	5	8	
16. Woman touches Christ's garment and is healed	9	5	8	
17. Two blind men healed	9			
18. Dumb demoniac healed	9			
S-29				
19. Feeding of 5,000	14	6	9	6
20. Walking on the sea	14	6		6
21. Syrophoenician's daughter healed	15	7		
22. Deaf and dumb man healed		7		
23. Feeding of 4,000	15	8		
24. Blind man in Bethsaida		8		
25. Demon cast out of boy (after transfiguration)	17	9	9	
26. Coin in fish's mouth	17			
F-29				
27. Man born blind cured				9
28. Demon cast out (Jesus accused of using evil power)			11	
29. Woman with spirit of infirmity (healed on Sabbath)			13	
SP-30				
30. Man with dropsy healed on Sabbath			14	
31. Lazarus raised				11
32. Ten lepers healed			17	
33. Two blind men cured at Jericho	20	10	18	

	Matthew	Mark	Luke	John
Final week				
34. Fig tree withered	21	11		
35. Malchus' ear restored			22	
Post-resurrection				
36. Second draught of fishes (Some post-resurrection appearances could be classified as miracles.)				21

APPENDIX N

NEARLY ALIKE OR SIMILAR EVENTS

The events that are similar are easy to confuse. Using dots on a chart will help you picture them chronologically, and there are no two dot patterns alike. If the events occurred at different geographical locations this will also help you to keep from confusing the events. It is also very interesting to trace and to note the frequency or build-up of certain reactions, miracles or teachings.

HEALING ON THE SABBATH

Jesus often came into conflict with the scribes and Pharisees because of His activities on the Sabbath. He had compassion on the sick, and the Bible records six occasions when He healed on the Sabbath (twice in both S-28 and F-29).

TWO REJECTIONS AT NAZARETH

The grace of God is demonstrated as Jesus returned to Nazareth the second time, even though they had tried to kill Him the year before. Because of their lack of faith in Him, all He did was heal a few people. He "marvelled at their unbelief."

202

MIRACLES ON THE SEA

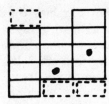

Jesus dramatically showed His supremacy over the created world twice on the Sea of Galilee. The first time He stilled the tempest on the sea, and the second time He walked upon the sea and gave Peter the power to also walk upon it.

GALILEAN TOURS OF JESUS

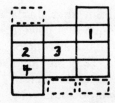

Jesus went on four preaching tours of Galilee:

1. In F-27 He appears to have been alone.
2. In SP-28 He took the four disciples with Him.
3. In S-28 He took the twelve apostles with Him.
4. In SP-29 He sent the twelve out two by two, and He also went.

CALLING DISCIPLES

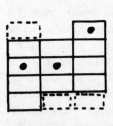

Jesus made His first five disciples in F-26 but they apparently did not stay with Him permanently. In SP-28 He called the four fishermen and Matthew, and they continued with Him. In S-28 He appointed from among His disciples twelve as apostles. A disciple was a learner or a follower; an apostle was one who was sent forth with a special commission (see Luke 9:1-5).

LONG DISTANCE HEALINGS

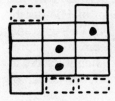

There were three times when Jesus healed someone at a distance so that He did not see the person. Two such healings occurred in Galilee, and one in the region of Tyre and Sidon.

203

HEALING THE BLIND

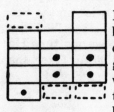

One of the most important miracles the Lord performed was the first healing of a blind man—the one who was also dumb and demon-possessed. It was here that the religious rulers made their decision that Jesus was not the Messiah but was working through evil powers. He also healed the blind in four other periods.

BLASPHEMOUS ACCUSATIONS

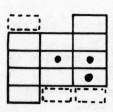

The blasphemous accusation that Jesus was doing His miracles through evil powers seems to have been the standard answer of the scribes and Pharisees. They couldn't deny His miracles, so when asked to explain them they said that it was through the prince of devils (Matt. 12:24). This accusation is recorded three times.

JESUS FORETELLS DEATH AND RESURRECTION

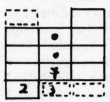

Jesus knew that He had come into the world to die and purchase salvation for man (Acts 2:23; Rev. 13:8). He stated it on the first appearance of His ministry in Jerusalem in S-27 and later in S-28. In S-29 He began to teach very plainly about His death: on the way to Mount Hermon, at the transfiguration, on the way down the mountain, and on the way back to Capernaum. In SP-30 after leaving Jericho on the way to Jerusalem and at the second anointing by Mary, He also told them of His death. In the final week He told them on Monday, Tuesday and Thursday, but His disciples just couldn't seem to comprehend it. Finally in the garden when the enemy came to arrest Him He said, "This is your hour, and the power of darkness" (Luke 22:53). They had attempted to kill Him for over two years (See Appendix Q).

MIRACLES IN JOHN

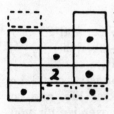

John records eight of Jesus' miracles in his gospel. He begins with His first and ends with His last, presenting the eight for a special purpose: "But these are written, that ye might believe that Jesus is the Christ, the Son of God; and that believing ye might have life through his name" (John 20:31).

SECOND COMING OF CHRIST

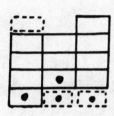

In S-29 after the apostles returned from the fourth Galilean tour and reported to Jesus that the people as a whole thought He was "John the Baptist, Elias, Jeremias or one of the prophets"—but not the Messiah—He began to tell them about His second coming. It was pictured at the transfiguration. In SP-30 after healing the ten lepers, He again told them and explained more about it in the parable of the pounds. In the final week He talked a lot about it in the Olivet discourse. In the upper room He added the new fact about His coming for the church. In the post-resurrection period while talking to Peter and John He again mentioned it: "till I come" (John 21:22).

In other parts of this book other similar events have been discussed or charted:
1. Angel activity (see Appendix A)
2. Casting out demons (see Appendix A and the period F-28)
3. Mountaintop experiences (see Appendix G)
4. Attempts to kill Jesus (see Appendix Q)
5. Feeding of 5,000 and 4,000 (both in S-29)

6. Healing lepers (SP-28 and SP-30)
7. Jesus and three immoral women (F-27, S-28 and F-29)
8. Voice from heaven (F-26, S-29, F.W.)
9. Cleansing the temple (S-27, F.W.)
10. Anointings of Jesus (S-28, SP-30)
11. Restorations from the dead (S-28, F-28, and SP-30)
12. Sending out the 12 and the 70 (SP-29, F-29)
13. Miracle of the fishes (SP-28 and P.R.)

Other aspects of the Lord's life and ministry could be traced or compared: healing ministry, social life, and so forth. This would be a profitable spiritual exercise for you when you complete this book.

YOUR NOTES AND REFERENCES:

APPENDIX O

Offerings and the Lamb of God

The first sacrifice was made in the garden of Eden when God prepared coats of skins for Adam and Eve. It does not tell what animal was used. Abel brought the firstlings of his flock as a sacrifice to God, and it was accepted. A ram, a male sheep, is among the animals offered by Abram in Genesis 15:9-21 when God made His covenant with him.

The word *lamb* first appears in relation to a sacrifice or offering in the account of Abraham being told to offer Isaac as a burnt offering. Isaac asked, "Behold the fire and the wood: but where is the lamb for a burnt-offering?" Abraham said, "My son, God will provide himself a lamb for a burnt-offering" (Gen. 22:7-8). Abraham bound Isaac and was preparing to kill him upon the altar, when God stopped him. Looking in the thicket he saw a ram caught by his horns. He "took the ram, and offered him up for a burnt-offering in the stead of his son" (Gen. 22:13). God did provide a lamb as a substitute.

When God prepared to take the children of Israel out of Egypt, the last plague was the plague of death of the firstborn. To protect His people He instructed them to take a lamb and kill it and sprinkle the blood on the doorposts (Exodus 12:3-13). This protected the household from the death angel. The Passover Feast was given to remind them of this deliverance, and a Passover lamb was sacrificed annually.

A lamb was also offered to redeem the firstborn of their flocks and families (Exodus 13:13). Each morning and evening the priests were to offer a lamb for the nation of Israel, and it was used in other sacrifices.

There are five basic ideas connected with the offering of a lamb in the Old Testament:

1. *Identification:* The one who brought the lamb laid his hands upon it and identified himself with it.

2. *Innocence:* The lamb itself was innocent of any wrong. It was to be without blemish. This pointed to the sinless Messiah.

3. *Substitution:* The lamb was a substitute for the person.

4. *Atonement:* The sins were covered until the time when "the Lamb of God" would pay the penalty in full.

5. *Redemption:* By the offering the people were redeemed or purchased from the guilt and penalty of sin (Exodus 13:13-15).

In the New Testament at the very beginning of Jesus' ministry, John the Baptist pointed Him out as the "Lamb of God" (John 1:29). Peter explains, "Forasmuch as ye know that ye were not redeemed with corruptible things, as silver and gold, from your vain conversation received by tradition from your fathers; but with the precious blood of Christ, as of a lamb without blemish and without spot" (I Peter 1:18-19). The Apostle Paul explains that Christ is our Passover (I Cor. 5:7). The offerings and sacrifices find their fulfillment in Him.

Luke mentions a trip to the temple after the birth of Jesus. Mary came to offer the sacrifice of purification. For a male child this was to take place forty-one days after birth. A lamb was to be offered, but if they couldn't afford a lamb they could offer a pair of turtledoves or young pigeons. (See Luke 2:22-25; Lev. 12:1-8; Exodus 13:2, 12, 15.) After Jesus healed the leper He told him to go and make the offering Moses commanded (Mark 1:44; Lev. 14:1-7).

After the destruction of Jerusalem in A.D. 70, the Jews quit offering a lamb at the Passover. The rabbis use as a substitute the dry shank bone of a lamb.

YOUR NOTES AND REFERENCES:

APPENDIX P

PARABLES

Jesus taught many things by the use of parables. The word *parable* comes from a Greek verb which means "to place by the side of." It has the idea of placing two things side by side for purposes of comparison. Normally the parable will be about common everyday things. The *known* will be used to help explain the *new* teaching. Some of the parables are misunderstood today because the things that were common are not familiar today. A knowledge of Jewish customs is very helpful. A parable will always have a little plot or story to it. There were other figures of speech used by the Lord. Jews were compared to salt (Matt. 5:13). This is a metaphor, but some figures of speech are so short that it is hard to classify them.

Some basic rules are necessary in the study of parables:
1. Don't try to establish doctrines from them. They are given to illustrate or explain doctrines that are clearly taught elsewhere in the Scriptures.
2. Each parable will be given to teach some particular truth. Sometimes the object or purpose of the parable will be stated at the beginning or end of it.
3. Look for just the principal points of the parable. Many details will be given to make the story complete.

Although Jesus had used parables before, He used the first large group in His discourse on the kingdom of heaven in F-28 (Matt. 13:1-53). The central theme in them was that there is going to be a period of time between the offer of the kingdom and the time it will be set up.

The next group of parables was given in F-29: the good Samaritan and the parables on service (Luke 10:25-37; 12:1—13:9). In the period of SP-30 Jesus taught on humility, rewards, excuses, discipleship, the lost sheep, the lost coin, the lost son and the lost job (Luke 14:7—16:18).

On Tuesday of the final week, the Lord gave many parables:

1. *Parables of rejection:* the two sons, the vineyard, the marriage feast and the wedding garment (Matt. 21:28—22:14)
2. *Parable of sign of His coming:* the fig tree (Matt. 24:32-41)
3. *Parables of readiness:* porter, thief, faithful servant and evil servant, and ten virgins (Matt. 24:42—25:13; Mark 13:33-37)
4. *Parables of judgment:* talents and the sheep and the goats (Matt. 25:14-46)

YOUR NOTES AND REFERENCES:

APPENDIX Q

QUARRELS OF SCRIBES AND PHARISEES

Nowhere is the wickedness of the human heart displayed more than in the accusations and quarrels the scribes, Pharisees and other Jewish leaders had with Christ. The first encounter occurred at the first cleansing of the temple, S-27. But they didn't seem to know what to do about Him.

The people in Nazareth attempted to *kill* Him in SP-28 (Luke 4:29). The scribes and Pharisees *accused* Him of blasphemy because He told the man let down through the roof that his sins were forgiven (Luke 5:21). They *mur-*

mured against Him for eating with publicans and sinners (Matt. 9:11).

In S-28 they *sought to kill* Jesus for breaking the sabbath and making Himself equal with God (John 5:16, 18). They *accused* Him of breaking the sabbath by plucking grain (Mark 2:24). They *watched* Jesus so they could *accuse* Him when He healed the man with the withered hand (Mark 3:2). The Pharisees and Herodians *plotted* how they could destroy Him (Mark 3:6). They *denied* that Jesus was a prophet for they said that if He were, He would not have let the sinful woman anoint His feet (Luke 7:39). They *accused* Him of casting out demons by the prince of devils (Matt. 12:24). Religious Israel, by the end of the summer, had decided that Jesus was not the Messiah but an evil man.

In S-29 they *disputed* with Jesus about hand-washing (Mark 7:5). They *tempted* Jesus by asking for a sign (Mark 8:11).

In F-29 back in Jerusalem, they said Jesus was *untaught* (John 7:15), and *sought to kill* Him (John 7:25). They *tried to arrest* Him but were unsuccessful (John 7:32, 45-46). They accused Him of *deceiving* the people (John 7:47). They brought a woman taken in adultery and tried to *trap* Him (John 8:3-6). They accused Jesus of being a *liar* (John 8:13). They tried to *stone* Jesus but were unable to (John 8:59). They called Jesus a *sinner* and declared that He had broken the sabbath because He had healed the man born blind (John 9:16, 24). Any who believed on Him were *threatened* and *mistreated* (John 9:22, 34). Jesus was accused of having a *demon* (John 10:20), and He was again accused of casting out demons by *evil powers* (Luke 11:15). They *provoked* and tried to *trap* Him (Luke 11:53-54). He was said to have *blasphemed* because He said He was the Son of God (John 10:33-36). Again, they unsuccessfully tried to stone Him (John 10:33, 39).

In SP-30 the Pharisees *derided* Him (Luke 16:14). They again took *counsel to kill* Him (John 11:53). Constantly

211

trying to trap Him, they tempted him on the divorce question (Matt. 19:3).

In the final week their anger mounted. They were *indignant* because the people praised Jesus at the triumphal entry (Matt. 21:15-16).

On Monday they *sought to destroy* Him (Mark 11:18) and *threatened* any who believed on Him (John 12:42).

On Tuesday they again tried to *trap* Jesus (Mark 12:13; Matt. 22:35-36). They sent *spies* and asked Him about paying tribute to Caesar. The religious rulers gathered and took counsel as to how they could take Jesus by *subtlety* again and *kill* Him for they were afraid of the people (Matt. 26:3-5). Finally, Judas agreed to *betray* Jesus for thirty pieces of silver (Matt. 26:14-16).

On Thursday night Judas with a great multitude from the chief priests, scribes, elders, temple guard and Roman soldiers *arrested* Jesus (Mark 14:43; John 18:3). His trials were a mockery (John 18:12-14, 19-24; Luke 22:66—23:25). Finally the extreme wickedness of the human heart demonstrated itself as man rejected and *crucified* his Saviour—the very God who created him (Mark 15:24). And this was by the most religious people of that generation. But evil had not won—Jesus came to die as a substitute for sinners (Rom. 5:8; I Peter 2:24).

Jesus, in the Sermon on the Mount in S-28, warned that the righteousness of the scribes and Pharisees was not sufficient (Matt. 5:20). He reminded them that they had rejected the message of John the Baptist (Luke 7:29-30).

In S-29 Jesus called them hypocrites (Mark 7:6). This word means "actors who are playing a part." The scribes and Pharisees were playing the part of being very religious. Jesus said their worship was vain and that they taught the doctrines of men and had left the commandments of God (Mark 7:7-8). They had made void the Word of God by their traditions (Matt. 15:6). Jesus warned His disciples against their teachings (Mark 8:15; Matt. 16:6, 12), and foretold that they would kill Him (Luke 9:22).

In F-29 Jesus told them that they didn't know the Father (John 8:19) and that their father was the devil (John 8:44). He condemned them as false guides (Luke 11:52) and hypocrites (Luke 12:1).

In the final week after He cleansed the temple the second time, Jesus said that they had made the temple a "den of thieves" (Matt. 21:13). He gave His most complete judgment of and warning against them in Matthew 23:1-36. He said that they:

1. Bound heavy burdens on men and did not try to help them (v. 4).
2. Did all their works to be seen of men (v. 5).
3. Exaggerated their pious dress (v. 5).
4. Desired the best places at the feasts (v. 6).
5. Coveted the chief seats in the synagogues (v. 6).
6. Loved greetings in the market place and to be called Rabbi, or master (v. 7).
7. Shut the kingdom of heaven against men (v. 13).
8. Devoured widows' houses (v. 14).
9. As a pretense made long prayers (v. 14).
10. Worked hard to make followers, then made them twofold more the child of hell than themselves (v. 15).
11. Were blind guides (v. 16).
12. Swore vainly (v. 16).
13. Made a great show of keeping the smallest commandments but omitted the important things (v. 23).
14. Were full of extortion and excess (v. 25).
15. Gave an outward appearance of being good, but their hearts were evil (vv. 27-28).
16. Were children of them that killed the prophets (vv. 29-32).
17. Were serpents, a generation of vipers (v. 33).
18. Would kill and persecute His messengers (v. 34).

The amazing thing is that Jesus Christ in His grace came to die for these people. Some Pharisees did receive Him. One notable example of a Pharisee who harassed and persecuted the believers was the Apostle Paul. No one is too great a sinner; all are invited to come; and Jesus promised that He will not cast out any who come (John 6:37).

YOUR NOTES AND REFERENCES:

APPENDIX R

Religious Parties

PHARISEES

There were three religious parties or sects among the Jews. None of the parties were very large. There were about six thousand Pharisees in the time of Christ. They would be classed as a conservative ritualist party and were more popular with the people because of their antiforeign attitude and high regard for the Scriptures. In the Sanhedrin, they held a majority. They held the oral law with its many interpretations and traditions to be just as binding as the Old Testament (see Appendixes O and Q). They went to great lengths to keep themselves separated from all that they considered unclean, and to perform all religious duties. Their great besetting sin was hypocrisy.

The Pharisees kept the Messianic hope alive, although their concept of the Messiah was perverted. They believed in a future state and the resurrection of the dead. They considered the common people as cursed because they did not know the law (Luke 18:9; John 7:49).

214

SADDUCEES

The Sadducees were the priestly party and were smaller in number than the Pharisees. They were mostly from wealthy influential priestly families. They were the rationalists of the day, only believing what they thought was reasonable. They denied the authority of the oral law, the resurrection, future punishment and rewards. (See Appendix J.) It is a paradox that these very same unbelieving priests were the ones who ministered in the temple and offered the sacrifices, yet as a class they didn't personally believe in the value or necessity of those sacrifices. It was their "business" that the Lord interfered with when He cleansed the temple. But Christ died for them too and "a great company of the priests were obedient to the faith" (Acts 6:7).

ESSENES

The New Testament does not mention the Essenes. They withdrew from ordinary society and lived near the Dead Sea. They practiced a monastic type of life. By adhering to an ascetic discipline and the simple life, they sought communion with God and purity of life. Because of the recent discovery of the Dead Sea Scrolls, some of which at least were deposited by them, they have become the object of recent study of archaeologists.

YOUR NOTES AND REFERENCES:

APPENDIX S

SANHEDRIN, OR COUNCIL

In New Testament times the Sanhedrin was the supreme civil and religious tribunal of the Jewish nation. The word that is usually translated "Sanhedrin" is also at times translated "council" (for example, Matt. 26:59; Mark 14:55; Luke 22:66). The Jews in their traditions liked to trace the history of the Sanhedrin all the way back to Moses' appointment of seventy elders but this has no real basis of fact. During the intertestament period the group was established in the form found in the gospel accounts.

The Sanhedrin had seventy-one members. Although authorities do not agree as to who belonged to the Sanhedrin it seems that it included (1) the high priest; (2) twenty-four chief priests who represented the twenty-four courses of the priesthood; (3) twenty-four "elders" who represented the people; and (4) twenty-two "scribes" who were interpreters of the law. The elders are sometimes referred to as rulers; at other times the word rulers is used for the whole Sanhedrin.

During the time of the Lord's ministry, the Sanhedrin met in a room on the south side of the temple called the "hall of squares." They met daily between the morning and evening sacrifices, except on the sabbath and feast days. Twenty-three men were required for a quorum. Jews recognized the jurisdiction of the Sanhedrin whether they lived in Palestine or in a foreign land. The Sanhedrin specialized in the interpretation and the application of both the written and the oral law (traditions) of the Jews. After the destruction of Jerusalem in A.D. 70 the Sanhedrin lost most of its power and finally ceased to exist in the fifth century.

The requirements for membership in the Sanhedrin were very strict. Each member must be a lineal descendant of Hebrew parents. He had to be well trained in Jewish laws. He needed to be familiar with the languages of surrounding nations. He had to have a good appearance, be modest and

216

free from haughtiness. He was required to be impartial at trial, and he had to take an oath to be fair and not to serve where there was enmity between himself and any prisoner that was to be judged.

YOUR NOTES AND REFERENCES:

APPENDIX T

TRIALS

PROCEDURES

The Sanhedrin was a final court of appeal whose purpose was to "save, not to destroy life." No man could be tried and condemned in his absence. Perhaps this is why Nicodemus said in F-29, "Doth our law judge any man, before it hear him, and know what he doeth?" (John 7:51). When the Sanhedrin took their vote they always started with the youngest member in order that junior members might not be influenced by the older members of the Sanhedrin. In cases of a capital offense the accused could be acquitted on the same day as he was tried, but a verdict of guilty had to be reserved for the following day. Because of this, trials could not commence on the day before the Sabbath or a feast. No criminal trial was started at night or carried into the night. The judges who condemned a criminal to death had to fast all day. After the sentence was passed, the condemned was not executed the same day on which the sentence was passed.

If there was enmity between a member of the Sanhedrin and a prisoner, the member was to disqualify himself and not sit as judge. The accusations were to be made before the trial began, not during the trial. No person could be found guilty on his confession alone. It was a unique ruling that if there was a unanimous verdict of guilty, they acquitted the prisoner. The Sanhedrin did not prove that Jesus was not the Son of God but they called His claim blasphemy. Jesus was struck and abused in the court contrary to law. And when He was brought before Pilate, the charge was changed. Pilate found him not guilty yet turned him over to be crucified. Roman law normally required a ten-day waiting period between the death sentence and the execution, but Pilate submitted to the pressure of the Sanhedrin and ordered Jesus crucified.

YOUR NOTES AND REFERENCES:

APPENDIX U

Universal Language: Greek

After Alexander the Great's world empire, Greek became the universal language, the language of culture. The Pharisees were opposed to Jews using it. The Old Testament had been translated into Greek (the Septuagint) in the intertestamental period.

Latin was the official Roman language, but it was not used by the Jews.

When they went into the Babylonian captivity the common people stopped speaking Hebrew. The Hebrew Scriptures were still read in the synagogues during the life of Christ, but they had to be interpreted into Aramaic. These Aramaic paraphrases were called Targums.

The language of the common people was Aramaic. It is related to Hebrew. It is called Hebrew in the New Testament (Mark 7:34; 15:34; John 19:20). The inscription on Jesus' cross was written in Latin, Greek and Hebrew (Aramaic).

YOUR NOTES AND REFERENCES:

APPENDIX V

VOCATIONS

LEVITES

The Levites were one of the twelve tribes of Israel. When Israel was worshipping the golden calf, the Levites remained true. God chose them to minister in holy things and help the priests (Num. 3:5-13). The priests were of the tribe of Levi, but only from the family of Aaron. When David divided the priesthood into twenty-four courses, he also divided the Levites into twenty-four courses (I Chron. 23:4, 28). They assisted the priests, had charge of the sacred vestments, utensils and provisions for offerings. David added to their duties those of being singers, musicians, porters and temple police (I Chron. 15:23; 25:6; Neh. 12:44).

PUBLICANS

The Romans farmed out their tax revenue for a province or district for a lump sum to companies. These in turn hired collectors which are called publicans in the New Testament. They were hated and despised by the people; they were social outcasts and often personally dishonest (Luke 15:1-2). Their offerings were not accepted in the synagogues.

Edersheim explains:

> The publicans also levied import and export dues, bridge-toll, road-money, town-dues, etc.; and, if the peaceable inhabitant, the tiller of the soil, the tradesman, or manufacturer was constantly exposed to their exactions, the traveller, the caravan, or the pedlar encountered their vexatious presence at every bridge, along the road, and at the entrance to cities. Every bale had to be unloaded, and all its contents tumbled about and searched; even letters were opened; and it must have taken more than Eastern patience to bear their insolence and to submit to their "unjust accusation" in arbitrarily fixing the return from land or income, or value of goods, etc. For there was no use appealing against them. . . . Another favourite trick of theirs was to advance the tax to those who were unable to pay, and then to charge usurious interest on what had thereby become a private debt.*

The Apostle Matthew and Zacchaeus were publicans. After Zacchaeus met the Lord, he promised to make restitution (Luke 19:8-9).

SCRIBES

One of the most important things you can learn about the times in which Jesus lived is the important position of the scribe. There are various names in the New Testament which refer to the scribes. They are called rabbis, teachers, lawyers and doctors. They were much more than secretaries. They spent their time studying the law and interpreting it to the common people. This was not only the written law but also

*Alfred Edersheim, *Sketches of Jewish Social Life* (Grand Rapids: Wm. B. Eerdmans Publishing Co., 1950), pp. 55-56.

the oral law which had been handed down by tradition. Often in the Scripture we see the scribes opposing Jesus in collaboration with the Pharisees, the chief priests, the Sadducees, and even the Herodians.

Cunningham Geikie says:

> So far as the Roman authority under which they lived left them free, the Jews willingly put all power in the hands of the Rabbis. They or their nominees filled every office from the highest in the priesthood to the lowest in the community. They were the casuists, the teachers, the priests, the judges, the magistrates, and the physicians of the nation. But their authority went still further, for, by the Rabbinical laws, nearly everything in daily life needed their counsel and aid. No one could be born, circumcised, brought up, educated, betrothed, married, or buried—no one could celebrate the Sabbath or other feasts, or begin a business, or make a contract, or kill a beast for food, or even bake bread, without the advice or presence of a Rabbi. The words of Christ respecting binding and loosing were a Rabbinical proverb: they bound and they loosed as they thought fit. What they loosed was permitted—what they bound was forbidden. They were the brain, the eyes, the ears, the nerves, the muscles of the people, who were mere children apart from them. . . .
>
> No Rabbi could take money for any official duty. . . . No teacher, preacher, judge, or other Rabbinical official, could receive money for his services. In practice this grand law was somewhat modified, but not to any great extent. A Rabbi might receive a moderate sum for his duties, not as payment, but only to make good the loss of time which he might have used for his profit. Even now it is a Jewish proverb that a fat Rabbi is little worth. . . . [Even] the greatest Rabbis maintained themselves by trades. . . .
>
> But there were ways by which even Rabbis could get wealth. To marry the daughter of one was to advance oneself in heaven; to get a Rabbi for son-in-law, and provide for him, was to secure a blessing. They could thus marry into the richest families, and they often did it. They could, besides, becomes partners in prosperous commercial houses.
>
> The office of a Rabbi was open to all, and this of itself secured the favour of the nation to the order. . . .

221

The central and dominant characteristic of the teaching of the Rabbis was the certain advent of a great national Deliverer—the Messiah, or Anointed of God. . . .

The prevailing idea of the Rabbis and the people alike, in Christ's day, was, that the Messiah would be simply a great prince, who should found a kingdom of matchless splendour. Nor was the idea of His heavenly origin at all universal; almost all fancied He would be only a human hero, who should lead them to victory. . . .

It was to a people drunk with the vision of such outward felicity and political greatness, under a world-conquering Messiah, that Jesus Christ came, with His utterly opposite doctrines of the aim and nature of the Messiah and His kingdom.†

YOUR NOTES AND REFERENCES:

APPENDIX W

WEDDINGS AND DIVORCE

WEDDINGS

Among the Jews there was a difference between the promise of marriage and the betrothal. A promise could be broken or set aside. A betrothal entered into was considered final. There was a difference between the betrothal and the wedding. The betrothal took place about a year before the wedding, but not over twelve months. The groom usually gave a letter or piece of money stating the betrothal. A legal document was signed fixing the dowry each brought. It was during the betrothal of Mary and Joseph that Mary was

†Cunningham Geikie, *Life and Words of Christ* (New York: D. Appleton & Co., 1880), I, 77-83.

found with child of the Holy Spirit (Matt. 1:18). On the day before the marriage the bride and groom fasted and confessed their sins in prayer as they would on the day of Atonement.

The groom with his attendants, singers or flute players went to the bride's house to get her, or sometimes they met on the way. They then returned to the house of the groom's father.*

The bride was veiled from head to foot in white with jewels and wreaths of myrtle leaves, and her hair was flowing (unless she was a widow), and she had on ointments and perfumes. The bride stayed with the women and did not join in the celebration until the feast was over (and then the veil was removed).

The wedding procession had the right of way over everything else on the road including funerals. If someone met a wedding procession, he was to join and go at least a short distance with them. Bridesmaids sang and danced before the bride on the way. The groom wore a crown, often of flowers (Song of Sol. 3:11). At the marriage the groom gave the bride a legal document, a Kethubah, in which he promised to work for her, to honor her, to keep and care for her, and to increase her money by half (by investing it).†

There was a ceremonial washing of hands, a benediction usually by the most important guest present, and then the marriage supper began.

At the marriage supper there were singing and music, riddles, and dancing. The celebration usually lasted from one to seven days, but sometimes went on until it wore itself out. Finally, the friends of the bridegroom led him to the bridal chamber where the friends of the bride had already taken her, and the wedding was consummated.

The wedding banquet was presided over by the ruler of the feast (John 2:8-9). It was his duty to take care of all

*Cunningham Geikie, *Life and Words of Christ* (New York: D. Appleton & Co., 1880), I, 473.

†Alfred Edersheim, *The Life and Times of Jesus the Messiah* (Grand Rapids: Wm. B. Eerdmans Publishing Co., 1945), I, 355.

the preparations. He gave thanks for the dinner, pronounced a benediction and acted somewhat the way a toastmaster does today.

CHRIST AND HIS BRIDE

Christ has entered into a marriage contract with His bride the church. The time will come when the church will depart from her home, this world, and Jesus Christ will meet her in the air (I Thess. 4:16-17) and take her to His Father's house.

Even as funeral processions were to give way to a wedding procession, so death must give way for the marriage of the Lamb (I Cor. 15:51-54). As the bride was veiled so that the people could not see her, even so the church will be taken so suddenly that the world will not understand what happened or be able to see her.

As the bride was dressed in jewels and other finery, so will the bride of the Lamb be clothed beautifully (Rev. 19:7-9; 21:9-21). The groom is described in Matthew 17:2.

DIVORCE

It is God's desire that marriage should never be broken (Gen. 2:24; Matt. 19:6). The marriage union is to be a type of the union of Christ and the church (Eph. 5:23-24, 27, 32). Because of the hardness of man's heart, God through Moses permitted the Israelites to divorce their wives if there had been fornication before the marriage was consummated. When Joseph found that Mary was going to give birth to a child, he supposed she had committed fornication. He planned to quietly give her a divorce, but the angel told him that the child was of the Holy Spirit.

The Pharisees' question in Matthew 19:3 was "Is it lawful to put away a wife for *every* cause?" Jesus' answer was no. In Greek there is a difference in the words for "fornication" and "adultery." The usual usage of "fornication" is sexual intercourse between unmarried people; "adultery" means sexual

224

intercourse between married people other than their own husband or wife.

YOUR NOTES AND REFERENCES:

APPENDIX X

CROSS AND PHYSICAL SUFFERING OF CHRIST

Jesus suffered much physical abuse before He was crucified:

1. An officer struck Jesus with his hand at the first trial before Annas (John 18:22-23).
2. At His second trial before Caiaphas, they spit in His face and buffeted Him. They blindfolded Him and then struck Him with the palms of their hands saying, "Prophesy, who struck you?" (Matt. 26:67-68; Luke 22:63-65).
3. Herod and his soldiers "set him at nought, and mocked him, and arrayed him in a gorgeous robe" (Luke 23:11).
4. At the second trial before Pilate, Jesus was scourged, then the soldiers placed a crown of thorns on His head and a purple robe on Him. They went up to Him shouting, "Hail, King of the Jews!" and struck Him with their hands (John 19:1-3).
5. After Pilate delivered Him to be crucified, the soldiers took Jesus and stripped Him and put a scarlet robe on Him. Putting a crown of thorns on His head and a reed in His hand, they mocked Him shouting, "Hail,

King of the Jews!" They spit on Him and took the reed and beat Him on the head (Matt. 27:27-30). He went out bearing His cross, but because He was weakened from the abuse He had suffered, they made Simon of Cyrene carry it for Him.

6. Arriving at Golgotha, "there they crucified him" (Luke 23:33). He endured six hours of intense suffering and thirst on the cross. The Bible does not give the details of this suffering, but secular history tells some of the horrors of crucifixion. However, the intensity of the physical suffering was overshadowed by the weight of the spiritual suffering as Christ cried out, "My God, my God, why hast thou forsaken me?" (Mark 15:34). At that time He suffered the equivalent of an eternity in hell for the whole world (I John 2:2), "that the world through him might be saved" (see John 3:16-18).

YOUR NOTES AND REFERENCES:

APPENDIX Y

GARMENTS

There were five basic pieces in the apparel of a person who lived during the life of Christ: (1) the inner garment, or tunic, (2) the girdle, or sash, (3) the outer garment, or mantle, (4) the headdress, and (5) the sandals.

TUNIC

The basic garment was the tunic. It was a shirt worn next to the skin, and in its simplest form was without sleeves. It was made of leather, haircloth, wool, linen or cotton, and it reached to the knees. The tunic of the rich would have sleeves and often reach to the ankles. Workers in hot weather would often wear only a tunic. The word *naked* is often used of men clad only in their tunic (John 21:7). The soldiers cast lots for the tunic of Jesus. This has often been called the robe; actually it was not the outer garment but the undergarment.

GIRDLE

The girdle was necessary to allow a person to work or walk freely in the loose-fitting tunic. It was either made of leather or of silk or of some other embroidered material. It was often used to carry money or other belongings. In Luke 12:35 Jesus said, "Let your loins be girded about." He meant be ready for action.

MANTLE

The outer garments, or mantle, was a large cloak which served as an overcoat, a shelter from the rain and a blanket at night.

HEADDRESS

The Jew always wore a turban in public. It was made of thick material and went around the head several times. It is very necessary in Palestine to protect the head from the sun.

SANDALS

The shoes the common people wore were a type of sandal that was fastened to the foot by leather thongs. John the Baptist mentioned not being worthy to loose the sandals of Jesus' feet (Mark 1:7).

There was a difference between men's and women's clothes although the basic design was the same. There is a definite exhortation in Deuteronomy 22:5 against men wearing women's clothing or women wearing men's clothing. The women usually wore a veil in public.

Jesus criticized the Pharisees for their hypocritical manner of dress. They placed very long fringes on the corners of their mantles (Matt. 23:5; Num. 15:37-38; Deut. 22:12). They wore large phylacteries. These were little containers which were fastened to the arm and the forehead by leather straps. They contained passages of Scripture which told of Israel's redemption from Egypt. The custom is based on the literal interpretation of Exodus 13:9, 16.

What kind of garments would Jesus have worn? Artists usually do not picture Him with a turban, but He doubtless wore one. His tunic is said to have been without a seam. His mantle was not white for the Bible says it became white when He was transfigured. Blue was a common color, or it may have been brown with white stripes. He would wear a girdle of some kind about his tunic; and John the Baptist speaks of His sandals. There is no mention of His wearing or using phylacteries.

There were four soldiers in the detail that crucified Jesus. They didn't want to tear His tunic into four parts, so they decided to cast lots for it (John 19:23-24). The word translated "coat" is the word for tunic, the inner garment. This was foretold in prophecy (Ps. 22:18).

YOUR NOTES AND REFERENCES:

APPENDIX Z

POLITICAL PARTIES

ZEALOTS

The Zealots were the national Jewish party which arose after the Romans took over Palestine in 63 B.C. They tried to arouse the people to fight for their deliverance. They were responsible for several minor clashes with Rome and were active in the final clash in A.D. 70 when Jerusalem was destroyed. In many cases they had degenerated into outlaw bands that terrorized the land. Barabbas was probably a Zealot. He was in prison for insurrection (Mark 15:7). The two thieves (correctly translated "robbers") that were crucified with Jesus may also have been Zealots (Matt. 27:44). One of Jesus' disciples was a Zealot, "Simon the Canaanite" (Matt. 10:4). "Canaanite" should be translated "Cananaean." This is the Aramaic name for Zealot.

HERODIANS

The Herodians were a small political party that was trying to further the power of the Herod family. Judaea and Samaria had been taken from Herod's control and were governed by a Roman procurator. The Herodians and Pharisees were bitter enemies, but they did conspire together to try to kill Jesus. Pilate and Herod Antipas were enemies until after the trials and death of Jesus (Luke 23:12).

YOUR NOTES AND REFERENCES:

REVIEW TEST NO. 1

One of the most helpful things you can do is mark your Gospels chronologically. This test is to see if you understand the chart and how to use your marked New Testament.

1. The ministry of Christ is divided into periods of about how many months? (check the best answer.)

   _____one year

   _____four months

   _____four weeks

2. The three periods: (1) from Christ's birth until He begins His ministry; (2) the final week; (3) the post-resurrection ministry, are all of different lengths of time. (True or False)

   _____T _____F

3. The vertical lines that divide the periods on the chart represent what three feasts? _____

   _____

4. If you want to find when an event happened, which direction do you look in the margin to find the date sign?

   _____forward

   _____backward

5. Using your marked New Testament, in what period did Jesus first cleanse the temple (John 2:14-16)? _____

6. In what period did Jesus feed the 5,000 (Mark 6:39-44)? _____

7. In what period was Jesus transfigured (Matt. 17:2)?

_____

8. The parable of the sower (Matt. 13:3)? _____

9. The parable of the fig tree (Luke 21:29)? _____

10. The man healed at the pool (John 5:5-9)? _____

The answers are given after the last test. Check yourself *after* you have taken the test. Don't cheat yourself out of the benefit of this exercise.

REVIEW TEST NO. 2

This test is over the introductory material and God's purpose in sending Christ.

There are six major themes traced in this book. List them:

1. _____

2. _____

3. _____

4. _____

5. _____

6. _____

7. Because of the rejection of the Messiah, two minor themes are introduced (minor in the sense of the amount of space devoted to them). What are they? _____

_____

The word *kingdom* is used in three different ways. What are they?

8. _____

9. _____

10. _____

REVIEW TEST NO. 3

This test is over the period that begins with Jesus' birth and extends until the beginning of His ministry.

1. Herod Antipas was king when Jesus was born.

    _____T _____F

2. Who first saw the Baby Jesus?

    _____wise men

    _____shepherds

    _____Simeon

3. What prophet foretold the place of the Messiah's birth?

    _____

4. How many of the religious rulers went to Bethlehem to see Jesus? _____

5. Who warned Joseph to flee to Egypt? _____

6. When Mary and Joseph returned from Egypt with Jesus, in what city did they make their home? _____

7. How old was Jesus when He went to the Passover Feast with Mary and Joseph? _____

Each person who reads about Jesus must decide who He is. (Here is a hint: Each of the possible three choices begins with an *l.*) List them:

8. _____

9. _____

10. _____

REVIEW TEST NO. 4

This test is over the period F-26.

1. Give the key word for this period. _____

2. John the Baptist had baptized only a few people before Jesus was baptized. _____T _____F

3. Jesus was led by the Spirit of God into the wilderness where He was tempted by Satan. _____T _____F

4. To save others from sin, a person must be sinless himself.

    _____T _____F

5. What weapon did Jesus use to meet the temptations of Satan? _____

6. Jesus was tempted in all points like we are.

    _____T _____F

7. When John the Baptist pointed to Jesus after His temptation, what did he call Him? _____

8. After talking to Jesus, Andrew went to find his brother. What was his brother's name and what did he tell him?

    _____

9. After Nathanael met Jesus, what three names or titles did he give Jesus? _____

    _____

10. At Jesus' baptism how were the three Persons of the Godhead revealed? _____

    _____

    _____

REVIEW TEST NO. 5

This test will cover SP-27, the two previous periods, and Appendix W.

1. What is the key word for SP-27? _____

2. What was the first miracle that Jesus performed? _____

   _____

3. The city of Cana is in Judaea. _____T _____F

4. A betrothal was considered as binding as marriage with the Jews. _____T _____F

5. About how long were a bride and groom betrothed before they were married? _____

6. When Joseph found that Mary was with child during this betrothal period, what was he going to do? _____

   _____

7. Who is to be the bride of Christ? _____

8. How many disciples met Jesus in F-26? _____

9. How far is Cana from Nazareth? _____

10. Who traveled with Jesus on His first journey to Capernaum? _____

    _____

    _____

REVIEW TEST NO. 6

This test is over the period S-27.

1. What is the key word for this period? _____

2. Although His followers did not understand it at the time, Jesus made a prophecy during this period. What was it about? _____

_____

3. What five words summarized Jesus' message to Nicodemus? _____

_____

4. Jesus did not perform any miracles in this period.

_____T _____F

5. Jesus cleansed the temple twice in His ministry.

_____T _____F

6. The purpose of Jesus' ministry was to bring condemnation on the guilty. _____T _____F

7. John the Baptist was imprisoned for what reason?

_____

8. Who had him put in prison? _____

9. What territory is Machaerus located in?

_____Galilee

_____Judaea

_____Peraea

10. Jesus and John both personally baptized followers.

_____T _____F

REVIEW TEST NO. 7

This test is on the period F-27.

1. What is the key word of this period? _____

235

2. Jews and Samaritans were usually good friends.

_____T _____F

3. The Galileans usually went to Jerusalem through Samaria.

_____T _____F

4. What did Jesus promise the woman at the well? _____

5. The Samaritans did not believe in the promise of a Messiah. _____T _____F

6. Jesus stayed for two weeks with the Samaritans.

_____T _____F

7. What is the name of the Samaritans' holy mountain?

_____

8. What is unusual about the healing of the nobleman's son? _____

_____

9. This is one of three miracles of healing that were given a special name in the text. What is the name? _____

10. On His first Galilean tour where did Jesus preach?

_____in the deserts

_____in the synagogues

_____in the market places

_____on the seashore

REVIEW TEST NO. 8

This test is over the period SP-28 and the synagogue in Appendix B.

1. What is the key word for this period? _____

2. What five disciples did Jesus call to follow Him in this period? _____

_____

3. The healing of the first demon-possessed man by Jesus occurred in this period.

   _____T _____F

4. To whom and to what city did Jesus send the leper He healed? _____

_____

5. How many disciples did Jesus take with Him on His second Galilean tour? _____

6. What relative of Peter did Jesus heal? _____

7. Besides healing, what miracle over nature did Jesus perform during this period? _____

8. What was Matthew's occupation? _____

9. What did Matthew do after he started following Jesus?

_____

10. Why was Jesus rejected by those of His own family and hometown? _____

_____

_____

REVIEW TEST NO. 9

This test is over the period S-28 and Appendix L.

1. What is the key word of this period? _____

2. On what day of the week did Jesus heal the sick man at the pool? _____

_____

3. What famous sermon did Jesus preach in this period, and what is the probable location where He gave it?

_____

4. How many apostles went on the third Galilean tour with Jesus? _____

_____

5. Who was the first person that Jesus restored to life?

_____

6. The city of Nain is located in

_____Galilee

_____Samaria

_____Judaea

7. What second long-distance healing occurred in this period? _____

_____

8. When the disciples plucked grain and ate it, what did the Pharisees say that they did wrong? _____

_____

9. What did Jesus do the night before He chose His twelve apostles? _____

_____

10. After He healed the demon-possessed, blind, dumb man, the Jewish leaders rejected Jesus' claim as Messiah and said that He was doing miracles by evil powers.

_____T _____F

REVIEW TEST NO. 10

This test is over the period F-28.

1. What is the key word of this period? _____

2. In what way did Jesus' teaching ministry change during this period? _____

   _____

3. John the Baptist, Jesus, and Jesus' disciples had been proclaiming that the kingdom of heaven (or kingdom of God) was _____.

4. In the kingdom of heaven parables Jesus taught what new thing? _____

5. What miracle did Jesus do that was connected with the Sea of Galilee? _____

6. How many demons were possessing the man who lived in the tombs? _____

7. How long had the woman been sick who touched Christ's garment? _____

8. How long had Jairus' daughter been dead when Jesus arrived? _____

9. The mourners were not sure that Jairus' daughter was really dead.

   _____T _____F

10. What did Jesus tell the demon-possessed man, who lived in the tombs, to do after He had healed him? _____

_____

REVIEW TEST NO. 11

This test is over all the key words and events studied through F-28. Give the key word for the following:

1. SP-27 _____

2. F-26 _____

3. F-27 _____

4. S-27 _____

5. S-28 _____

6. SP-28 _____

7. 5 B.C.—A.D. 26 _____

Give the key word for the period of each event:

8. The baptism of Jesus _____

9. The woman at the well _____

10. The first leper healed _____

11. The man let down through the roof _____

12. The first anointing of Jesus' feet _____

13. The wise men worship Jesus _____

Give the time period when each of the following events took place:

14. The nobleman's son healed _____

15. The first rejection of Jesus at Nazareth _____

16. The temptation of Jesus _____

17. Changing water to wine _____

18. Jesus' first Galilean tour _____

19. John the Baptist imprisoned _____

20. Man with the withered hand healed _____

REVIEW TEST NO. 12

This test is over the period SP-29, the Galilean tours, and the life of John the Baptist.

1. What is the key word for this period? _____

2. The first rejection of Jesus at Nazareth took place in this period.

_____T _____F

Give the time periods and the number of disciples that went on the Galilean tours with Jesus:

3. First tour _____ _____

4. Second tour _____ _____

5. Third tour _____ _____

6. Fourth tour _____ _____

Tell what event or activity happened to John the Baptist in the following periods:

7. About 4 or 5 B.C. _____

8. S-26 _____

9. F-26 _____

10. S-27 _____

11. S-28 _____

12. SP-29 _____

REVIEW TEST NO. 13

This test is over the period of S-29.

1. What is the key word for this period? _____

2. Which came first, the feeding of the 4,000 or the feeding of the 5,000? _____

3. When did Jesus walk on the water, before or after the feeding of the 5,000? _____

4. What was the name of the discourse given by Jesus in the synagogue at Capernaum? _____

5. Jesus performed His third long-distance healing in this period; whom did He heal? _____

6. At His transfiguration, who were the two men that appeared and talked with Jesus? _____

7. What did they talk about? _____

   _____

8. After the fourth Galilean tour, the disciples reported that most of the people were accepting Jesus as the Messiah.

   _____T _____F

9. Who did Peter say Jesus was? _____

   _____

10. On what mountain was Jesus probably transfigured?

    _____

REVIEW TEST NO. 14

This test is over the period of F-29.

1. What is the key word of this period? _____

2. What is the name of the feast that this period begins with? _____

3. This period ends with what feast? _____

4. In John 8 what discourse did Jesus give? _____

   _____

5. What chapters in what two books record the events of this period? _____

6. This period records the healing of a man born blind; why were the Pharisees angry about his healing?

   _____

   _____

7. What did the Jews do to the blind man who was healed?

   _____

8. Why did Jesus say He had come (John 10:10)? _____

   _____

9. What two things did Jesus say about the safety of the believer in John 10:28? _____

   _____

10. The Jews attempted to stone Jesus in this period but were unable to.

    _____T _____F

REVIEW TEST NO. 15

This test is over the key events through period F-29. Give the period in which each occurs:

1. The first anointing of Jesus _____

2. Temptation of Jesus _____

3. Death of John the Baptist _____

4. First cleansing of the temple _____

5. Peter's mother-in-law healed _____

6. Jesus stills the tempest on the sea _____

7. Feeding of the 5,000 _____

8. Kingdom of heaven parables _____

9. Parable of the rich fool _____

10. Apostles sent out two by two over Galilee _____

11. Parable of the good Samaritan _____

12. First rejection at Nazareth _____

13. Coin in the fish's mouth _____

14. Woman who touched Christ's garment _____

15. Sermon on the Mount _____

16. Jesus talked to Nicodemus _____

17. First leper healed _____

18. Demon-possessed, blind, dumb man healed _____

19. Transfiguration _____

20. Third Galilean tour _____

REVIEW TEST NO. 16

This test is over the period SP-30.

1. What is the key word for this period? _____

2. In teaching about the rich man who died, the Lord revealed that after death the lost will be conscious, remember the past, and be in torment.

    _____T _____F

3. Lazarus the beggar was the brother of Mary and Martha.

_____T _____F

4. How long was Lazarus dead before Jesus restored him to life? _____

5. How many lepers did Jesus heal in this period? _____

_____

6. In what other period did Jesus heal a leper? _____

_____

7. What title did the blind men use in calling to Jesus for help? _____

8. The Jews not only wanted to kill Jesus but also _____

_____

9. Who anointed Jesus' feet in this period? _____

10. In what other period did a woman anoint Jesus' feet?

_____

REVIEW TEST NO. 17

This test is over Bible geography. Give the name of the town in which or near which the key event occurred:

1. Lazarus raised from the dead _____

2. Water changed to wine _____

3. Man let through the roof _____

4. Home of the woman at the well _____

5. Birthplace of Jesus _____

6. Temple cleansed _____

7. Jairus' daughter raised _____

8. Peter's mother-in-law healed _____

9. Zacchaeus climbed a tree _____

10. Matthew called as a disciple _____

11. Light of the world discourse _____

12. Bread of life discourse _____

13. Place where John the Baptist was imprisoned _____

14. Widow's son raised from the dead _____

15. Second anointing of Jesus' feet _____

16. The city where Jesus was when He healed the noble-
    man's son _____

17. The city in which the nobleman's son was healed

    _____

18. Man at the pool healed _____

19. First demon-possessed man healed _____

20. New birth discourse _____

REVIEW TEST NO. 18

This test is over Appendix G.

1. The mountain of temptation was probably near the Sea
   of Galilee.

   _____T _____F

2. About what mountain did the woman at the well talk
   to Jesus? _____

3. The Sermon on the Mount was probably preached on
   what mountain? _____

4. Jesus was transfigured on Mount Ebal.

_____T _____F

List the four natural divisions of the land of Palestine.

5. _____

6. _____

7. _____

8. _____

9. About how many aerial miles is it from the Sea of Galilee to the Dead Sea? _____

10. About how many miles does the Jordan River wind from the Sea of Galilee to the Dead Sea? _____

REVIEW TEST NO. 19

This test is over Appendixes G and H.

1. To what country was Jesus taken to escape the wrath of Herod the Great? _____

2. The meaning of Decapolis is "ten cities."

_____T _____F

3. Philip II ruled Samaria.

_____T _____F

4. Herod Antipas ruled what two countries? _____

_____

5. Pilate began to rule the same year that Jesus began His ministry.

_____T _____F

247

List the three blots on the record of Herod Antipas:

6. _____

7. _____

8. _____

9. Herod the Great was born in what country? _____

10. As a memory help we have given nicknames to the kingdoms during the ministry of Christ. List the ruler and nickname of each kingdom:

Judaea and Samaria _____ _____

Galilee and Peraea _____ _____

Ituraea _____ _____

REVIEW TEST NO. 20

This test is over the events of the F.W. (final week) period. Give the day upon which the event occurred:

1. Jesus cleansed the temple _____

2. Jesus rode the colt into the city _____

3. Fig tree cursed _____

4. Olivet discourse given _____

5. Sadducees question Jesus about the resurrection _____

6. Jesus' arrest _____

7. Jesus' trial before Pilate _____

8. Jesus questioned about paying tribute _____

9. Last supper of Jesus with His disciples _____

10. Upper room discourse _____

REVIEW TEST NO. 21

This test is over the P.R. (post-resurrection) period.

1. An angel rolled away the stone from the tomb so Jesus could come out.

   _____T _____F

2. In His resurrection body, Jesus ate food.

   _____T _____F

3. In His resurrection body, Jesus could pass through doors and walls into a locked room.

   _____T _____F

4. Jesus was seen by how many of His followers after His resurrection? (Check best answer.)

   _____eleven

   _____fifty

   _____over 500

5. Jesus appeared (at different times) to His followers in more than one geographical place.

   _____T _____F

6. Jesus' post-resurrection ministry with His disciples lasted

   _____ten days _____forty days _____fifty days

7. What were the disciples to do after Jesus left? _____

   _____

8. What new ministry were His followers to have? _____

   _____

9. From what place did Jesus ascend to heaven? _____

10. What promise did the two men in white apparel (angels) give after the ascension? _____

_____

REVIEW TEST NO. 22

This test is over all the key events in all the periods. Give the period in which each event occurs.

1. Lazarus raised from the dead _____

2. First rejection of Jesus at Nazareth _____

3. Kingdom of heaven parables _____

4. Fig tree cursed _____

5. Woman at the well _____

6. Third Galilean tour _____

7. Sermon on the Mount _____

8. Walking on the water _____

9. Baptism of Jesus _____

10. Death of John the Baptist _____

11. Twelve apostles chosen _____

12. First leper healed _____

13. Swine run into the sea _____

14. Olivet discourse _____

15. Second miraculous draught of fishes _____

16. The seventy sent out two by two _____

17. Feeding of the 5,000 _____

18. Second anointing of Jesus _____

19. Stilling the tempest on the sea _____

20. Transfiguration _____

REVIEW TEST NO. 23

This test is over Appendix N, similar events. Place the time periods after each series.

1. Two rejections of Jesus at Nazareth _____, _____

2. Miracles on the sea _____, _____

3. Long-distance healings _____, _____, _____

4. Calling of the disciples and appointing of the apostles

   _____, _____, _____

5. Galilean tours _____, _____, _____, _____

6. Healing of lepers _____, _____

7. The two anointings of Jesus _____, _____

8. The two cleansings of the temple _____, _____

9. Miracles of the fishes _____, _____

10. Restorations from the dead _____, _____, _____

11. Voice from heaven _____, _____, _____

12. Jesus and immoral women _____, _____, _____

13. Sending out the twelve and the seventy two by two

    _____, _____

14. Feeding of 5,000 and 4,000 _____, _____

15. Eight miracles in John _____, _____, _____,

    _____, _____, _____, _____, _____

REVIEW TEST NO. 24

This test is over all the Appendixes.

1. The Pharisees were a political party.

    _____T _____F

2. About how many Pharisees were there during the ministry of Christ? _____

3. The Zealots wanted to free the Jews by force of arms.

    _____T _____F

4. The Pharisees disliked sitting in the chief seats in the synagogue.

    _____T _____F

5. In the synagogue the men and women sat together.

    _____T _____F

6. The dead were usually buried on the same day that they died.

    _____T _____F

7. The Jews, during the New Testament period, reclined while eating their meals.

    _____T _____F

8. The Sadducees believed it was very important to keep the oral law as well as the written law.

    _____T _____F

9. Scribes were sometimes called lawyers or doctors of the law.

    _____T _____F

10. Jewish men usually wore a turban or head covering.

    _____T _____F

REVIEW TEST ANSWERS

REVIEW TEST No. 1: (1) four months; (2) True (30 years, one week, and forty days); (3) Feast of Passover, Feast of Tabernacles and Feast of Dedication; (4) backward; (5) S-27; (6) S-29; (7) S-29; (8) F-28; (9) F.W.; (10) S-28.

REVIEW TEST No. 2: (1) Jesus revealing what God is like; (2) Jesus revealing through His life God's perfect standard for men; (3) Jesus providing redemption from sin; (4) Jesus destroying the works of the devil; (5) Jesus offering the kingdom to Israel; (6) Jesus being received and rejected as Messiah; (7) Jesus' second coming and the establishment of the church; (8) the *realm* or territory ruled; (9) the *people* that are ruled; (10) the *reign* or rule itself (time).

REVIEW TEST No. 3: (1) False—Herod the Great; (2) shepherds; (3) Micah 5:2; (4) none of them; (5) an angel (God through an angel); (6) Nazareth; (7) 12; (8) a lunatic; (9) a liar; (10) the Lord.

REVIEW TEST No. 4: (1) SEE; (2) False; (3) True; (4) True; (5) the Word of God; (6) True—Hebrews 4:15; (7) the Lamb of God; (8) Peter: "We have found the Messias, which is, being interpreted, the Christ" (John 1:41); (9) Rabbi, the Son of God, the King of Israel (John 1:49); (10) God the Son was being baptized, God the Holy Spirit descended on Him in a form like a dove, and God the Father spoke from heaven.

REVIEW TEST No. 5: (1) C.C.; (2) Changed water to wine; (3) False—Galilee; (4) True; (5) about a year; (6) put her away (divorce her); (7) the church (II Cor. 11:2; Eph. 5:25-32); (8) five; (9) about five miles; (10) His mother, brothers and disciples.

REVIEW TEST No. 6; (1) FFNJJ; (2) about His death and resurrection (John 2:19-22); (3) "Ye must be born again"; (4) False (John 2:23); (5) True; (6) False (John 3:17); (7) He publicly reproved Herod Antipas for living with his brother's wife; (8) Herod Antipas; (9) Peraea; (10) False—Jesus did not.

253

REVIEW TEST No. 7: (1) WELL; (2) False; (3) False—the Jordan Valley; (4) living water; (5) False—they had some perverted ideas concerning Him but they believed in the promise; (6) False—two days; (7) Gerizim; (8) Jesus was separated from the son by about twenty miles; (9) long-distance healings; (10) the synagogues.

REVIEW TEST No. 8: (1) BLDG.—; (2) Peter, Andrew, James, John and Matthew; (3) True; (4) to the priest in Jerusalem; (5) four; (6) Peter's mother-in-law; (7) miracle of the fishes; (8) publican (tax collector); (9) Made a feast and invited his friends so that they could meet Jesus; (10) They did not believe that one they knew so well could have such unusual power (Mark 6:3-6).

REVIEW TEST No. 9: (1) MAN; (2) the Sabbath; (3) Sermon on the Mount, Horns of Hattin; (4) twelve; (5) the widow's son at Nain; (6) Galilee; (7) the centurion's servant; (8) breaking the Sabbath by reaping and threshing grain; (9) He prayed; (10) True.

REVIEW TEST No. 10: (1) SEA; (2) He began to teach in parables; (3) at hand; (4) that there would be a delay between the preaching of the kingdom and the actual establishment of it territorially; (5) He stilled the tempest; (6) a legion (6,000); (7) twelve years; (8) not long; she had just died; (9) False—they were sure she was dead; (10) to go home and tell his friends what Jesus had done for him.

REVIEW TEST No. 11: (1) C.C.; (2) SEE; (3) SEA; (4) FFNJJ; (5) MAN; (6) BLDG.—; (7) BABIES; (8) SEE; (9) WELL; (10) BLDG.—; (11) BLDG.—; (12) MAN; (13) BABIES; (14) F-27; (15) SP-28; (16) F-26; (17) SP-27; (18) F-27; (19) S-27; (20) S-28.

REVIEW TEST No. 12: (1) 212.; (2) False—the second; (3) F-27, probably none; (4) SP-28, four; (5) S-28, twelve; (6) SP-29, twelve—two by two; (7) his birth; (8) began his ministry; (9) Baptized Jesus; (10) parallel ministry with Jesus in Judaea and imprisoned by Herod Antipas; (11) Sent messengers to inquire of Jesus; (12) He was beheaded by Herod.

REVIEW TEST No. 13: (1) FOOD; (2) 5,000; (3) after; (4) bread of life; (5) Syrophoenician's daughter; (6) Moses and Elijah; (7) His coming death; (8) False; (9) "Thou art the Christ, the Son of the living God" (Matt. 16:16); (10) Mount Hermon.

REVIEW TEST No. 14: (1) SERVING; (2) Tabernacles; (3) Dedication; (4) light of the world; (5) John 7–10 and Luke 10–13; (6) He was healed on the Sabbath; (7) Questioned him and cast him out of the synagogue; (8) "that they might have life, and that they might have it more abundantly"; (9) They will never perish and no one can pluck them out of His hand; (10) True.

REVIEW TEST No. 15: (1) S-28; (2) F-26; (3) SP-29; (4) S-27; (5) SP-28; (6) F-28; (7) S-29; (8) F-28; (9) F-29; (10) SP-29; (11) F-29; (12) SP-28; (13) S-29; (14) F-28; (15) S-28; (16) S-27; (17) SP-28; (18) S-28; (19) S-29; (20) S-28.

REVIEW TEST No. 16: (1) TRAVEL; (2) True; (3) False; (4) four days; (5) ten; (6) SP-28; (7) Son of David, a title of the Messiah; (8) Lazarus; (9) Mary; (10) S-28.

REVIEW TEST No. 17: (1) Bethany; (2) Cana; (3) Capernaum; (4) Sychar; (5) Bethlehem; (6) Jerusalem; (7) Capernaum; (8) Capernaum; (9) Jericho; (10) Capernaum; (11) Jerusalem; (12) Capernaum; (13) Machaerus; (14) Nain; (15) Bethany; (16) Cana; (17) Capernaum; (18) Jerusalem; (19) Capernaum; (20) Jerusalem.

REVIEW TEST No. 18: (1) False—near the Dead Sea; (2) Mount Gerizim; (3) Horns of Hattin; (4) False—Mount Hermon; (5) seacoast plain; (6) mountain range; (7) Jordan Valley; (8) eastern tableland; (9) 65 miles; (10) 200 miles.

REVIEW TEST No. 19: (1) Egypt; (2) True; (3) False—Ituraea; (4) Galilee and Peraea; (5) True; (6) He stole his brother's wife; (7) Killed John the Baptist; (8) Jesus was brought to trial before him; (9) Idumaea; (10) Judaea and Samaria—Pilate, Ice Cream Cone Kingdom; Galilee and Peraea—Herod Antipas, Bow Tie Kingdom; Ituraea—Herod Philip II, Teacup Kingdom.

REVIEW TEST No. 20: (1) Monday; (2) Sunday; (3) Monday; (4) Tuesday; (5) Tuesday; (6) Thursday; (7) Friday; (8) Tuesday; (9) Thursday; (10) Thursday.

REVIEW TEST No. 21: (1) False—to show that it was empty; (2) True; (3) True; (4) over 500; (5) True; (6) forty days; (7) Wait in Jerusalem for the promise of the Father (Holy Spirit); (8) They were to be witnesses of Christ to every creature unto the uttermost part of the earth; (9) Mount Olivet; (10) That Jesus would return to earth again in like manner as they had seen Him go.

REVIEW TEST No. 22: (1) SP-30; (2) SP-28; (3) F-28; (4) F.W.; (5) F-27; (6) S-28; (7) S-28; (8) S-29; (9) F-26; (10) SP-29; (11) S-28; (12) SP-28; (13) F-28; (14) F.W.; (15) P.R.; (16) F-29; (17) S-29; (18) SP-30; (19) F-28; (20) S-29.

REVIEW TEST No. 23: (1) SP-28, SP-29; (2) F-28, S-29; (3) F-27, S-28, S-29; (4) F-26, SP-28, S-28; (5) F-27, SP-28, S-28, SP-29; (6) SP-28, SP-30; (7) S-28, SP-30; (8) S-27, F.W.; (9) SP-28, P.R.; (10) S-28, F-28, SP-30; (11) F-26, S-29, F.W.; (12) F-27, S-28, F-29; (13) SP-29, F-29; (14) both S-29; (15) SP-27, F-27, S-28, S-29, S-29, F-29, SP-30, P.R.

REVIEW TEST No. 24: (1) False—a religious party; (2) 6,000; (3) True; (4) False; (5) False; (6) True; (7) True; (8) False—it was the Pharisees who insisted upon keeping the oral law; (9) True; (10) True.